# THE IMPACT OF
# THE RAILWAYS
# TO EAST ANGLIA

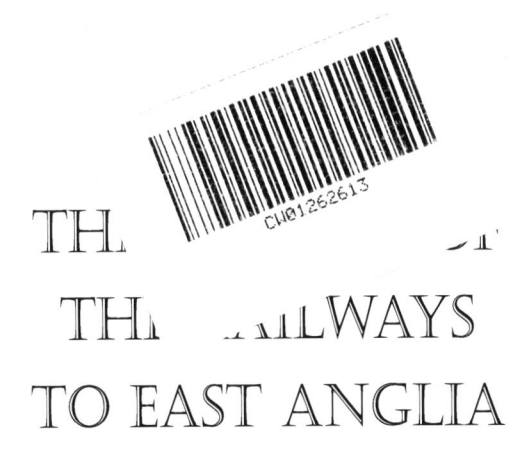

JOHN GALE

Published by

**MELROSE BOOKS**

An Imprint of Melrose Press Limited
St Thomas Place, Ely
Cambridgeshire
CB7 4GG, UK
www.melrosebooks.co.uk

**FIRST EDITION**

Copyright © John Gale 2015

The Author asserts his moral right to
be identified as the author of this work

Cover designed by Melrose Books

**ISBN 978-1-910792-10-0**

All rights reserved. No part of this publication may be reproduced, stored in a retrieval system, or transmitted, in any form or by any means electronic, mechanical, photocopying, recording or otherwise, without the prior permission of the publishers.

This book is sold subject to the condition that it shall not, by way of trade or otherwise, be lent, re-sold, hired out or otherwise circulated without the publisher's prior consent in any form of binding or cover other than that in which it is published and without a similar condition including this condition being imposed on the subsequent purchaser.

Printed and bound in Great Britain by:
4edge Limited
7a Eldon Way, Eldon Way Industrial Estate
Hockley, Essex
SS5 4AD

# Table Of Contents

| | | |
|---|---|---|
| INTRODUCTION | | v |
| 1 | THE RAILWAY NAVVIES | 1 |
| 2 | EARLY EAST ANGLIAN STATIONS | 8 |
| 3 | ENGINE DRIVERS AND GUARDS | 16 |
| 4 | FREIGHT | 24 |
| 5 | SIGNALLING | 30 |
| 6 | PLATELAYERS | 37 |
| 7 | HOTELS AND SEASIDE HOLIDAYS | 44 |
| 8 | ACCIDENTS | 67 |
| 9 | CARRIAGES AND LOCOMOTIVES | 75 |
| 10 | PASSENGERS | 82 |
| 11 | LEVEL CROSSINGS | 88 |
| 12 | INDUSTRIAL RELATIONS | 94 |
| 13 | THE LONDON TERMINI | 100 |
| 14 | STRATFORD WORKS | 107 |
| | APPENDIX 1 | 110 |
| | APPENDIX 2 | 111 |
| | APPENDIX 3 | 113 |
| | APPENDIX 4 | 114 |
| NOTES | | 116 |
| BIBLIOGRAPHY | | 124 |

# MAP OF THE
# GREAT EASTERN RAILWAY
## AND LINES IN CONNECTION

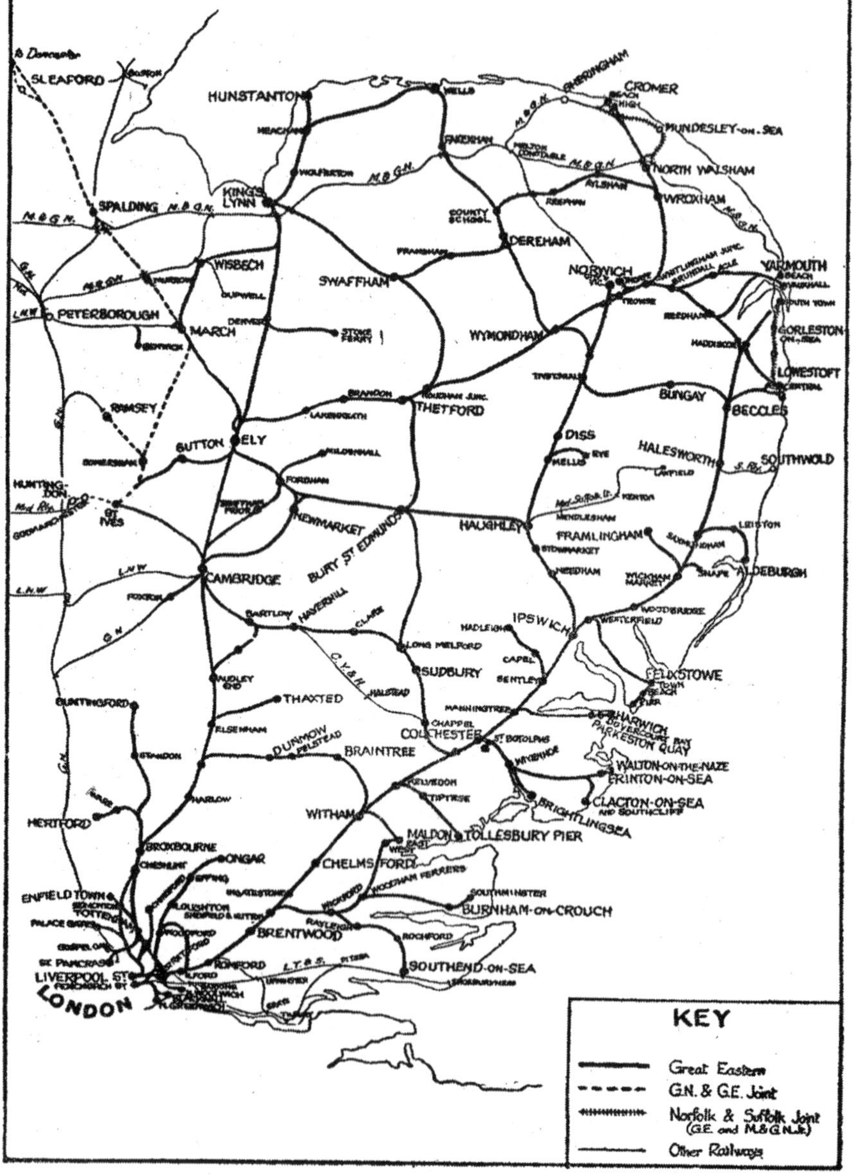

# Introduction

East Anglia was not attractive to railway speculators. Predominantly agricultural in nature, and relatively isolated from other counties, it was not considered to be an area that would generate high profits for shareholders. It was therefore not surprising that the railway age was late in arriving in this part of the British Isles. However, when the early East Anglian railway companies eventually began to operate, they brought immediate changes to rural life. Firstly, there was a significant increase in the mobility of the population. People who usually travelled no further than ten miles from home during a lifetime could now, if they had money, reach other East Anglian towns or even travel as far as London. Secondly, there were better employment opportunities, especially for agricultural labourers who could earn higher wages as railwaymen. Trade in livestock, grain, fruit, vegetables, and fish was boosted by the ability of producers to get their produce to market quickly, relatively cheaply and, most importantly, whilst still fresh. Trains also enabled visits to be made to the seaside. It was usual for the public to visit East Anglia's resorts on excursions as day trippers; however, some people stayed for longer holidays. These visits proved to be a financial benefit to East Anglian coastal resorts, causing significant growth in their populations.

This book looks at the development of East Anglian railways during the 19th century, and the work undertaken by railwaymen in a dangerous but disciplined environment. Many of the quotations given in the book are taken from local newspapers obtained from either the Ipswich Records Office or the British Library. Information has also been obtained from early copies of the *Great Eastern Magazine*, and other books and periodicals that give details of the early East Anglian railway companies. The information on the Wells Station accident is taken from the Alan Summers Collection, and the memorial to two railwaymen is taken from a tombstone in the South Porch of Ely Cathedral.

Prints and photographs used to illustrate the text have been obtained from the National Railway Museum, the Science & Society Picture Library, Enfield Libraries, Grace's Guide, Robert Humm, Fred Spalding, Curzon Studios, Spitalfields Life, and the Star Series of postcards.

All avenues have been pursued in obtaining permission to publish. However, in the event of a permission being omitted, please write to the publisher so that the relevant page can be rectified.

# 1

# THE RAILWAY NAVVIES

The Parliamentary Acts of Enclosure that were passed between 1760 and 1820 brought about major changes in the organisation of family labour.[1] Rural workers, no longer able to rely upon agriculture as a source of income, were forced to find alternative means of remuneration, and many of the agricultural labourers chose canal construction in order to earn a living wage. Between 1758 and 1801, no fewer than 65 Acts of Parliament were passed for making or extending canals in order to accommodate the need for faster and cheaper methods of transportation. At the end of that period, canals extended over 3,000 miles, and had cost upwards of 13 million pounds.[2] The labourers employed in this construction work became skilled in the use of the pickaxe and shovel, and were referred to as 'navigators'. This term, in an abridged form, was adopted in the 19th century by the men who built the railways. They were called 'navvies'.

East Anglia, because of its rural nature, was not considered to be a lucrative proposition for railway speculators. Consequently, it was not until 1836 that an Act authorising the construction of a railway line from London to Norwich and Yarmouth via Ipswich was granted to the Eastern Counties Railway. However, financial difficulties caused construction work to be halted at Colchester in 1843. When in 1845 a further railway line was opened between Norwich, Yarmouth and Cambridge the towns of Thetford and Brandon became the first Suffolk towns to be served by a railway; however, it was not until 1846 that the Eastern Union Railway extended the line from Colchester to Ipswich, and then on to Yarmouth. The construction of these railways brought navvies to East Anglia. They were itinerant workers who travelled great distances on foot in order to find work on railway sites. The work was hard and dangerous, and although it was well paid it was intermittent. The men had only picks, shovels, and gunpowder to carry out their work, and many men lost their lives as a result of the casual attitude towards safety that prevailed on 19th century construction sites.

## THE COMING OF THE RAILWAYS TO EAST ANGLIA

When their shifts were completed, the navvies lived in settlement camps, where living conditions were appalling. Drunkenness and rioting were commonplace after the monthly pay was distributed, and such behaviour caused consternation and fear in the villages through which they passed. In due course navvies gained a reputation for violence, immorality, and anti-social behaviour, which in 1846 led Thomas Carlyle to write that "I have not in my travels seen anything uglier than that disorganic mass of labourers, sunk three-fold deeper in brutality by the three-fold wages they are getting".[3] In 1862 the *Ipswich Journal* reported that:

> "In consequence of the construction of the Colne Valley Railway we have had an influx of railway labourers, and continual scenes of disorder… Last Sunday week I am told that drunken navvies were parading the street in parties of four and five together, their conduct and language was most disgraceful, they accosted any female they happened to meet, and the knowledge that there is but one Constable and no "lock-up" gives them a perfect license and impunity… Not long since the Inspector was attacked between 12 and one at night by a party of eight or nine whom he had just turned out of a public house, and who beat and kicked him violently… On Sunday last several ladies were afraid to leave the Churchyard at Haverhill in consequence of the violent conduct of the navvies."[4]

However, the worth of navvies was often recognised by their employers. The main contractors for railway construction in East Anglia were Samuel Morton Peto and Thomas Brassey. Both of these men valued the work carried out by their navvies. Peto placed strict control on the sale of alcohol on his sites, and he also developed the idea of sick clubs for his workmen. He also used his navvies to assist his campaign to be elected as Member of Parliament for Norwich in 1847. However, when the navvies became involved in a number of riots in the town centre, Peto was forced to pay the sum of £70 to cover the damage they had caused.[5] Thomas Brassey paid the highest wages of all the railway contractors, and was renowned for looking after the interests of his men. When men were sick or injured he helped them financially, and if they died he helped their dependants. Brassey was held in high esteem by all who worked for him, and when, in 1870, it was learned that his death was imminent, navvies travelled from all parts of Britain to wait outside his home in the hope of seeing him one final time.[6]

Most of the 19th century railway contractors preferred to sub-contract some sections of the works to small gangs of navvies. Thomas Brassey supplied his sub-contractors with all the necessary materials and plant, leaving them to contract for the manual labour alone.[7] Brassey was successful because he took care to ensure that the price agreed for each item of work was fair; however, sometimes when a contract was going badly the sub-contractor absconded and the men were not paid at all. In *Bridging the Years*, Charles Matthew Norris gives the following description of the average sub-contractor during the years of 'Railway Mania'.

> "Any man with ambition and quite slender financial backing could become an employer of navvy labour on small railway contracts, and by behaving like most others 'on the make' at that time, honestly or somehow, could make a profit which was likely to be multiplied many times before the fever of speculation was over."[8]

Such men gave no consideration to the welfare of their fellow workers. The navvy was wanted only as long as his strength remained, and at the end of a contract he was often discharged "penniless, discontented, reckless, and deteriorated in mental and bodily condition".[9]

The methods used for the excavation of cuttings for the railways in East Anglia resulted in many unnecessary deaths and injuries. It was usual to undercut the faces of cuttings to enable the ground above to collapse. The spoil could then be shovelled into wheelbarrows that were then pulled to the top of the cutting to be tipped. This was achieved by means of a rope tied to a horse at the top of the cutting, the wheelbarrows being guided up wooden planks by a 'runner'. These methods were particularly dangerous – both for the men undertaking the excavation work, as the ground often collapsed on top of them before they could vacate the undercut areas, and also for the 'runners' who guided the barrows up the wooden planks, as they often slipped in wet weather, and were crushed by the fully laden wheelbarrows. The use of explosives for the excavation of tunnels was in its infancy, and consequently deaths often resulted because the navvies were not given sufficient time to move to a safe distance from a gunpowder explosion. Fortunately, only two tunnels were constructed in East Anglia; the Stoke tunnel located to the south of Ipswich railway station, and the Cromer tunnel, built by the Norfolk and Suffolk Joint Railway now abandoned. No deaths resulted from the use of explosives whilst these tunnels were being constructed.

It was usual for navvies to work shifts both during the daylight hours, and at night, and consequently extraordinary rates of progress were achieved. Over a period of six months in 1857, 800 navvies excavated 350,000 cubic yards of earth and 45,000 cubic yards of ballast for the construction of the East Suffolk railway. During this time 90 tons of iron girders were also fixed, 17 cuttings were completed, and several timber and iron bridges were nearing completion.[10] Sometimes unexpected finds were encountered in the excavations:

> "As railway workers on the Colchester Stour Valley Line were excavating the line at Gt Cornard, nearly opposite the Five Bells Inn, they discovered, 12ft from the surface, a large tooth and a tusk, 4ft in length of the mammoth or fossilized elephant.
> 
> Last week, labourers upon the line at Mt Bures discovered about 5ft below the surface, four amphorae about 3ft high and very small at the neck, one was taken out perfect and another with a handle and spike broken off, the other two were broken. Another implement was found with two outer prongs and having double points upon which are knobs of brass similar to which are placed on the horns of cattle."[11]

In 1846 a Select Committee was appointed "to inquire into the Condition of the Labourers employed in the Construction of Railways, and other Public Works, and into the Remedies which may be calculated to lessen the peculiar Evils, if any, of that Condition".[12] From a study of the evidence presented to the Select Committee it is apparent that considerable importance was attached to the provision of religious instruction for navvies. This was considered to be essential as navvies were generally held to be irreligious.

One witness described navvies as "very vile and immoral characters… the most neglected and spiritually destitute people I ever met".[13] The religious ideology prevalent in the 19th century held that the spiritual welfare of the individual was more important than the provision of material needs, and the Select Committee noted with approval that the contractor, Samuel Morton Peto, distributed bibles to his navvies. Peto told the Committee "nothing is charged for it … Whenever a man asks for a bible he has it".[14]

The Select Committee were also concerned at the prospect of railway work being carried out on a Sunday, thereby limiting the amount of time available for religious instruction. The idea of working on a Sunday was abhorrent to the Victorian middle class, and it was not unusual for railway companies to receive petitions from offended parishioners complaining about the desecration of the Sabbath and the consequent effects upon the servants of the company. When it became apparent that Sunday work was being carried out whilst the Eastern Union railway was under construction, the Mayor of Colchester personally intervened. As Chief Magistrate he personally ordered the contractors to stop work, and threatened to issue summonses against any ganger whose men were found to be doing Sunday work within the borough boundary.[15] In 1850 the *Bury & Norwich Post* reported that:

> "The Sunday train from Sudbury has been discontinued to the gratification of the inhabitants, it was opened for the accommodation of the graziers in sending cattle and sheep to the Monday market. Being so near St Peter's Church and at the time of starting during the afternoon service and the noise and cruelties exercised on the poor beasts in getting them into trucks it was greatly annoying."[16]

The likelihood of a railway being constructed in a rural area often elicited an unfavourable response from both landowners and residents. Most landowners were reluctant to give up their land to a railway company if they believed that they were unlikely to receive adequate compensation. The local residents, however, were more frightened by the thought of large numbers of navvies rampaging through their villages. A typical letter from a tenant to his landowner concerning railway construction is set out below:

> "My Lord,
> I have received a notice (as occupier) from the Solicitors in a projected railway from Stowmarket to Sudbury, requesting my dissent, assent, or neutrality thereto. This line if accomplished would pass over four fields belonging to your Lordship in the Parish of Combs, on the north side of Combs Church, and about a quarter of a mile therefrom.
>
> As I conclude your Lordship will not favour this (in my opinion) unsatisfactory line, I have, as occupier, sent in my dissent which can be withdrawn if your Lordship should so wish.
>
> I remain,
> My Lord
> Your Lordship's Most obedient Servant
> John Kirby Moore
>
> P.S I open my letter just to inform your Lordship that Mr Boby has had a notice respecting a railway from Stowmarket to Wymondham in Norfolk, which would pass over Columbine Hall Farm. I required him to dissent which he will. Your Lordship has undoubtedly been applied to from the projectors of both the railways mentioned in this letter."[17]

Carrying out survey work for a prospective railway was also likely to elicit a hostile response from residents.

> "I have again been insulted and annoyed for some days past, by Railway vagabonds trespassing upon my lands surrounding this house, damaging the herbage and crops, and insulting me – a resident owner upon an estate which I inherited from my mother and her ancestors… We had good roads and good conveyances upon them, and Railway monopoly was not wanted to add to the distresses of the country, by throwing people out of their occupations and employment."[18]

Despite the initial hostility towards railways, when rails were finally fixed in place and locomotives began to appear, the inhabitants served by the new railway were happy to indulge in lengthy celebrations. It addition to local dignitaries, it was customary for the navvies who had built the railway to be present on these occasions. In August 1849, when the Eastern Union Railway was within six-and-a-half miles from Norwich, an excursion was arranged through the countryside between Burston and Flordon. A party of gentlemen from Norwich and surrounding areas, together with 100 workmen, set out to travel from Flordon to Diss and back. Villagers and navvies lined the route to cheer the train as it passed. Flags and banners were hoisted in Flordon, and Mr Parry, the contractor for eight miles of the line, entertained the company most liberally at his shanty on Flordon-green.[19]

A previous ceremony, held in 1847 to celebrate the laying of the foundation stone for the Chappel viaduct on the Sudbury line, had unexpected consequences for the organisers. The navvies, dressed in their traditional white frocks and straw hats, paraded to the point where the stone was to be fixed. The chairman and vice chairman of the company then mounted a platform, and using two silver trowels, buried a bottle containing a newly minted sovereign, a shilling, a sixpence, and a four penny piece, before fixing the stone into position. The 200 people present then adjourned to a nearby marquee for refreshments. Only hours after the ceremony had taken place the stone was removed and the bottle stolen. The coins were subsequently handed to a barmaid in the nearby 'Rose and Crown', an action that led to the arrest of William Coates, a bricklayer from Norwich. Although Coates was prosecuted at the Quarter Sessions for the theft of £1, 11s, 10d the case was dismissed because sufficient evidence was not available to prove the prisoner guilty.[20]

# 2

# Early East Anglian Stations

The railways came late to East Anglia, but eventually they were to have a great effect upon rural life in the towns and villages. Trains increased the mobility of people, and they offered a faster and cheaper means of transport for manufactured goods and farm produce. The railways soon displaced the older modes of road transport in East Anglia that relied upon the use of an antiquated road system. They also were able to compete on favourable terms with vessels carrying goods either by river, or along the coast by sea. The provision of a railway station therefore became a necessity for rural communities, and consequently a variety of station buildings appeared across East Anglia. These ranged from the rural halt for the use of villagers, to elegant Victorian structures built to serve more important towns. Many of the smaller stations were remote from the places that they purported to serve, a situation that was summarised poetically:

> "Melancholy places where none but Great Eastern trains deign to stop,
> And there's no one to pick up and no one to drop."[1]

The tiny station of Wolverton, however, became famous in 1862 when the Sandringham Estate was purchased by the Prince of Wales. Located near to the 'Big House', Wolverton became the station for Royalty and other members of high society to descend when arriving by train. Between 1884 and 1911 645 Royal trains were dealt with at Wolverton. Queen Victoria arrived in 1899, the German Emperor in 1902, King Carlos of Portugal in 1902, King of the Hellenes in 1905, the Dowager Empress of Russia in 1907, the Queen of Portugal in 1907, and the King and Queen of Spain in 1907.

"Each Christmas the red-carpeted platform would be gaily decorated with greenery, gift-laden tree and Royal bunting to welcome regular Royal gatherings. Chattering house parties would descend for Edwardian sporting weekends at the Big House. Less frequently, a garlanded honeymoon train would arrive. But for pomp and circumstance, nothing could match a state visit by a foreign monarch or a Royal funeral occasion."[1A]

The intermediate stations on the Ipswich to Bury St Edmunds railway of 1846 were expensive to construct, and Bury St Edmunds, Stowmarket, and Needham (later Needham Market) stations are particularly fine examples of railway architecture, being an elaborate mix of Tudor and Jacobean features.[1B] An equally elaborate station was built at Maldon in 1848 for the Maldon, Witham and Braintree Railway, and the initials 'MWB' appear at the top of the station downpipes. This company was quickly taken over by the Eastern Counties Railway, and late in the 19th century the name of the station was changed to Maldon East Station. It is a particularly grand structure for a branch line, with large Dutch gables, a nine bay arcade across the front, a cast iron imitation stone balustrade, and tall stone mullion windows.[2] When the Great Eastern Railway eventually became responsible for East Anglia's railways it adopted a shield upon which the town of Maldon is shown. However, the Eastern Counties Railway sometimes economised on station construction. When a branch line to Enfield was opened in 1849, the company adapted an old Georgian mansion to serve as the new Enfield station.[3]

In contrast to the grandeur of some of the main line East Anglia stations, the halt at Wilby consisted of a single platform on which were sited a freight wagon body and a small hut. The station was located near to Stradbroke on the Mid-Suffolk Light Railway, and because it was miles from anywhere, services were infrequent and passengers were scarce.[4] Around 60 men were employed in the line's heyday. Each station was staffed by one 'signal porter', except for Stradbroke where there was a station master as well as a clerk to deal with finance.[5]

From their inception the railways offered secure and relatively well paid employment, and consequently many agricultural labourers ceased working on the land and instead sought employment on the railways.

There were considerable opportunities available, particularly at the larger stations, where railwaymen served in a variety of occupations. A station master was responsible for the porters, parcel clerks, freight clerks, ticket office staff, and maintenance workers required to run the station efficiently. In addition, at many stations arrangements were made for the distribution of milk to surrounding areas, and for the storage of coal. The smaller country stations in East Anglia invariably required fewer staff. However, near to the rural station of Melton Constable a railway works was opened that specialised in the construction of steam engines and the repair of carriages. The works not only employed people from Melton Constable, but it also offered opportunities to people living in the surrounding villages.[6]

Because the railway station provided such a useful service to the nearby towns it was customary for the local traders and gentry to provide an annual supper for the railway employees. At Eye in 1885 a supper was held at the White Lion Hotel where, as the *Ipswich Journal* reported:

> "Mrs Rowling as usual did her very best to make us happy, by placing a good turkey at the top of the table, a fine joint of beef at the bottom, and a prime leg of mutton in the centre; and from these, with the usual *et ceteras* – not forgetting a bountiful supply of good malt liquor – we made 'a right good meal'."[7]

The station master usually presided at these annual events. He was an important person within a community, and because he came into frequent contact with the local gentry he was considered to have the same status as a doctor or clergyman. It was possible for an able candidate to rise through the ranks to become a station master, but the route was a lengthy one, which entailed on-the-job learning about all aspects of station work. A station master was required to have had experience in all of the posts necessary for the running of a station, and to have served at several stations before being appointed. As befitting his position, a station master wore an elegant uniform with gold braid, and most carried a watch in a fob pocket in order to check the timings of trains. He was often allocated a house near to the station premises for his family, and this was necessary for he was expected to be on call continuously. The career of Charles

Edward Banyard with the Great Eastern Railway, which is set out below, appears in *Railway Ancestors* by David T Hawkings:

> Great Eastern Railway Company
> Superintendent's Department; Salaried Staff Register
> Date of Entry    4/2/89
> Age at Entry     16
> Charles Edward BANYARD

| GRADE | STATION | PAY | DATE |
|---|---|---|---|
| Probationary Clerk | Aldeburgh | 6/- | 4/2/89 |
| Lad Clerk | " | 10/- | 1/12/90 |
|  | " | 12/- | 29/2/92 |
|  | " | 14/- | 6/3/93 |
|  | " | 16/- | 12/3/94 |
|  | " | 18/- | 4/8/97 |
| Goods Clerk | Eye | 20/- | 14/11/98 |
|  | " | 22/- | 14/12/99 |
| Goods Clerk | Leiston | 23/- | 15/10/00 |
|  |  | 24/- | 31/12/00 |
|  |  | 25/- | 31/12/01 |
| Second Parcels Clerk | Ipswich | 28/- | 4/1/04 |
| District Relg. Bkg Clerk* | " | 25/- plus expenses | 19/12/04 |
| District Relg. Bkg Clerk (Station Master 14/10/13) | " | £70 plus expenses | 23/7/07 |
|  |  | £75 plus expenses | 1/9/08 |
|  |  | £80 plus expenses | 1/1/11 |
|  |  | £85 plus expenses | 1/1/14 |
|  |  | £90 plus expenses | 1/4/15 |
| Station Master | Thurston | £100 plus house | 1/2/16 |
|  |  | £110 plus house | 1/1/18 |
|  |  | £120 plus house | 1/7/19 |
| Station Master (4th Class) | " | £230 + £23 FB | 1/8/19 Rent £23 Bonus £5 1/4/20 £25 1/7/20 |
|  |  | £230 + £18 FB | 1/7/21 |

\* Relieving Booking Clerk
FB Fixed Bonus[8]

Main line railway stations, unlike their rural counterparts, were busy places. People were constantly arriving and departing from the station forecourt, often travelling in the branch stagecoaches which, in the early days, were necessary to convey passengers to and from the surrounding areas. If the station had a goods yard the station master was required to carry out frequent checks in order to ensure that everything was in order. A horse was often used at larger stations if shunting operations were required, for a horse was economical to use as it cost £1 per week to keep, rather than the cost of 6/- per hour for a steam engine.[9] However, shunting on the main line could be a dangerous business. William Sparrow was moving three trucks with two horses on the down main line at Stowmarket, and together with the horses, he was walking in the space between the two main lines when one of the horses was struck by a passing coal train. The horse was killed and Sparrow was dragged to the ground, subsequently dying from his injuries.[10]

Most stations had a garden that required daily attention from the staff. A well-kept garden enabled the station to compete in the annual station garden competition with the aim of winning a prized first class certificate to hang in the station entrance hall.[11] There were also other maintenance tasks that had to be carried out daily. Toilets needed to be cleaned and oil lamps had to be maintained in good working order. However, gas lighting soon began to replace oil lamps on the Eastern Counties Railway.

> "Mr John Thompson, of this place, having completed his contract with Messrs Peto & Betts, for lighting the Beccles station platform and goods shed with gas, they were generally illuminated for the first time on Thursday, the 8th inst. to receive a special train of visitors from Halesworth to hear the 'English Glee and Madrigal Union' at the Assembly rooms."[12]

It was also necessary for the station premises to be decorated periodically, and outside contractors were usually appointed for this work. The *Ipswich Journal* gives details of an 1847 court case in connection with outstanding payment due for work undertaken at Bentley station. The case is of interest because the cost of the work carried out was published. The price for papering and varnishing three rooms at the station is given as £12, 17s, 2d, and this price included the cost of all materials.[13] Sometimes the stations erected were of a temporary nature, the buildings being abandoned when the railway line was extended after a few years. This was the case at Loughton, where the original station opened in 1856, but only existed until 1865.[14]

It was necessary for workmen to be extremely careful when carrying out maintenance work near to passing trains. At Needham Market station it became necessary to place a large door in position at the goods shed. The door was three inches thick, and measured 14ft high and 10ft wide, with a weight of about half a ton. Henry Jarman, a Carpenter employed by a local building firm, attempted, with seven other men, to place the door in position. However, as they were manoeuvring the door a train from Stowmarket ran through the station at speed, and generated a wind that blew the door to the ground. Jarman was trapped beneath the door, but was released and taken to the East Suffolk and Ipswich Hospital where he spent the next six weeks. However, his injuries were serious, and he eventually died at his home.[15]

Sometimes accidents resulted because of the negligence of railway staff. When in October 1850 the engine on a train from Bury to Ipswich failed, the two carriages were towed to Haughley Junction by four horses for a replacement engine. The horses were accompanied by two Station Masters who climbed onto luggage which had been piled onto the roof of the carriages. The horses were withdrawn near to Thurston station, and the carriages were then coupled to a replacement engine. However, the two Station Masters remained seated on luggage on the roof of the carriages with their backs to the engine. Inevitably when the train passed beneath a bridge they were struck by the brickwork arch, and both men were killed.[16] A further act of negligence, which could have resulted in a very serious accident, occurred at Loughton station on 28th June 1857:

> "Porter Clarke and Foreman Porter Rudder were each fined a day's pay for failing to couple together properly two carriages on the 9am train from Loughton. Presumably complaints of rough riding led to an examination at Stratford, when it was found that the carriages were only held together by the side chains."[17]

The delivery of milk was an important function of the early railways. Milk could be delivered for a distance of up to 15 miles by road and horse, and still remain fresh. However, carriage by rail was cheaper than any other method, and because it was only necessary for a horse to draw the milk churns from the railway station, the animal was still fresh enough to be put onto a milk round.[18] The milk churns each held 204 quarts and were conical in shape. Because they were extremely heavy it was necessary to tilt a churn on one side and then to roll it along. It required two porters to move the churns from their point of storage on the station platform into the milk vans. Beccles station on the East Suffolk line had a movable platform bridge that enabled milk churns to be moved onto the up platform for onward transit.[19]

Railways were also ideal for the delivery of coal to East Anglian stations, the coal being brought either by sea to local ports, or from other parts of the country. It was usual for a coal merchant to rent space in the station yard, and sometimes a siding was provided for the storage of wagons. A small country coal yard would receive perhaps three or four wagon loads a week, whilst a yard serving a built-up area might get through ten wagon loads a day.[20]

In 1875, coal merchants at Great Yarmouth brought a case against the Great Eastern Railway. The coal merchants complained that the Great Eastern Company charged more for the carriage of seaborne coal from Yarmouth than for coal brought overland from Peterborough. They argued that the Great Eastern Company preferred overland routes to seaborne coal as overland routes were more profitable. Although their argument was not accepted, the Company had not complied with a previous order to "afford all reasonable facilities for loading trucks directly from the ships," so the applicants were awarded one-half of their costs, to be paid by the Company.[21]

Every station employed clerical staff in order to complete the large amount of paperwork that was required on a daily basis. Everything had to be handwritten, and periodically officials from Head Office would call to inspect the invoices, way bills, and ledgers that the clerical staff produced. It was not unusual for people to be fired if their written work was not of a satisfactory standard. Booking office staffs were required to keep a record of tickets issued, and tickets sold, and they were also responsible for ordering adequate supplies of tickets from the printers for future use. It was not unusual for letters to appear in newspapers complaining about the carelessness or dishonesty of the booking clerks, who apparently often gave deficient change. However, a letter published in *The Graphic* pointed out that booking clerks were not all bad, as the writer had given a sovereign in mistake for a shilling, and had the good luck to get the balance returned to him by post immediately he notified the station of the error.

# 3

# ENGINE DRIVERS AND GUARDS

The Eastern Counties railway was the first railway to be constructed in East Anglia, and it soon acquired an extremely poor reputation. The service was so appalling that by 1860 it was being described in the following terms:

> "Notoriously there is no railway system in the Empire so badly worked as the Eastern Counties. There is no system on which the Passenger Trains are so few or so irregular; none on which the rates for Passengers and Goods are so excessive; and few, if any, where accidents are more plentiful."[1]

The Directors of the railway made a bad start by adopting a 5ft gauge, instead of the 4ft 8.5 inches gauge recommended by their engineer, John Braithwaite. When in 1843 it became necessary to convert the railway to the standard gauge, 84 miles of track needed to be converted at a cost of £1,000 per mile.[2] The slowness of the early Eastern Counties trains became a subject for public derision, and caused one irate passenger to send the following letter to the company:

### "A CHALLENGE
### SENT TO THE DIRECTORS OF THE EASTERN COUNTIES RAILWAY COMPANY

**GENTLEMEN,**
Your engines seem to be taking it very easy. I have an old **Donkey** that I will guarantee to best some of your **Business Trains** in speed. For example, your Time Table allows 6, 7, and 8 Minutes from Cheshunt to Waltham. Now, I will back my old Donkey to do it in 4 MINUTES, and thus leave me time to get my breakfast before the Train starts.

This little Donkey is 15 years old, or I would back him to run against some of your Trains from Cheshunt to London. I know he could have beaten them 4 or 5 years ago, and I think he might do so now, but I am not willing to tax the powers of my old friend. He will do what I have stated with ease, and have a good bray afterwards, as if in contempt of the INFERIOR POWER of **Eastern Counties Steam.** If you are willing to accept the Challenge, name the day, and have an umpire on a fast horse to see all fair, and I will be ready for you.

> I am Gentlemen,
> Your humble Servant,
> GEORGE HOY"[3]

The early steam engine was not easy to drive, and both driver and fireman needed to be constantly on the alert to avoid accidents. Engines had no continuous brakes until the introduction of the Westinghouse braking system in the 1880s, so the driver could only use the engine brake and rely upon the guard to apply his screw down brake in order to stop. No windshields were fitted to the early engines to protect the driver and his fireman, so conditions on the footplate were dreadful in foul weather, and visibility was extremely limited. When, eventually, windshields were fitted, it became possible to see the line ahead through the two circular glass openings in the shield, but no proper protection was offered to the engine crew until engine cabs were introduced into locomotive design later in the 19th century. Some enginemen were against the introduction of enclosed engine cabs because the forward vision of the driver was restricted. This view was shared by I. K. Brunel, who argued that pampering the locomotive crew with a cab would lead to accidents. Brunel was also against the education of drivers, as he considered that illiterates would pay more attention to their duties.[3A]

The early locomotives used on the Eastern Counties and Eastern Union railways were supplied by a variety of firms. They were mainly 2-2-2 tank locomotives, bought from either Sharp Brothers of Manchester, Stohert & Slaughter of Bristol, or R & W Hawthorn of Newcastle. Some larger 2-4-0 long boiler locomotives were supplied to the Eastern Counties Railway by the Robert Stephenson Company.[4]

The drivers for these engines were mostly experienced men, poached from rival railway companies. Most of them were under 30 years of age, and some were no doubt strike breakers who had been forced to leave their previous driving jobs due to the hostility of their fellow workers. For many young men the usual route to becoming a driver was to join the railway company as an engine cleaner, a filthy job which involved removing dirt, soot, grease and grit from the most inaccessible places on a locomotive. The next step was to progress to fireman and, after a considerable amount of learning on the job, the passed fireman eventually became a driver. It was not an easy route; progression to driver could take many years, and only a few of the aspiring young men were eventually chosen.

Trying to maintain balance on a vibrating footplate whilst operating the regulator, or trying to feed coal into the firebox, was both tiring and dangerous.

> "The balance of the early locomotives was far from perfect and they were liable to rock dangerously when travelling at speed. To overcome this unsteadiness Fernihough, of the Eastern Counties, in the 40s, tried weighting the wheels to compensate for the weight of the upper works. His experiment was completely successful, the balanced engines proving capable of achieving high speeds in complete safety. One of them, a ten-year-old Stephenson 'long boiler' of 'North Star' design, reached 70 miles an hour in 1856, beating by three miles the speed record held by the Great Western's 'Great Britain'.[5]

It was essential for drivers to thoroughly know the routes they had to follow. The location of every signal, level crossing, or prominent landmark had to be memorised. This knowledge was vital for night driving, and even more so in dense fog or snow when it became quite easy for both driver and fireman to become disorientated. Great reliance was placed upon oil lamp signals, and throughout most of the 19th century an oil lamp showing a white light was used to signify a clear road.

"White is right, red is wrong
Green means gently go along."[6]

This could be dangerous, as in an intense snowstorm a coating of snow on the red spectacle glass of an oil lamp could make the lamp appear to show white light. This defect was partially responsible for a frightful train crash at Abbots Ripton on the East Coast route in January 1876. However, despite the loss of life in this accident, it was not until 1892 that the Board of Trade insisted that green light should be used to indicate 'all clear' instead of white light.[7]

Some accidents on the early railways were as a result of mistakes made by either the engine driver or his fireman. On a September afternoon in 1847, an Eastern Counties Railway down luggage train had just passed Broxbourne station when the fireman decided that the engine needed to be oiled. Despite being against company regulations, he began clambering over the moving engine with an oil can to oil the moving parts. Whilst undertaking this dangerous practice he lost his grip and was thrown onto the rails, and consequently the moving locomotive and the train passed over him, cutting off both his legs. He was taken to a London hospital, but whether he survived the ordeal or died of his injuries is not recorded.[8]

Driver error caused a major accident at Wells Station on the Great Eastern in May 1879. The approach to Wells station was downhill for the last two miles from Warham Crossing, with the following gradients:

    1,230 yards rising one in 166
    420 yards falling one in 76
    100 yards falling one in 440
    1,560 yards falling one in 85
    135 yards falling one in 226

The 7.50am train from Norwich was being driven by John Phillips, a driver with 23 years' experience. He was driving his usual engine, a Great Eastern 2-4-0 tender locomotive built by Neilson & Co. in 1867. His fireman, Alfred Robert Collins, had four years' experience and had worked with Driver Phillips for a period of 13 months. The train consisted of six carriages and a van, and was two coaches longer than usual. The train passed a 15mph speed sign at the top of the bank at 26mph, and because of the additional weight the brake was applied. However, this was not sufficient to slow the train so the driver whistled to the Guard to apply his brake and then he put his engine into reverse gear. This was still not sufficient to slow the train, but the brakes had been tightly screwed down, and when the train passed the Gatekeeper at Stiffkeys Crossing, sparks could be seen flying from the wheels of the tender and from the wheels of the Guard's van. The train finally ran into the station and broke the buffer stops, smashed through 10ft of wooden platform, a 14 inch wall separating the water closets from the platform, and two party walls. The engine had travelled a distance of 30ft and in doing so had killed Mr George Cooke, a coachman who happened to be in the porters' room. The Inspecting Officer attributed the accident to the fact that the driver had allowed his train to attain too great a speed when descending the bank into Wells station. He therefore recommended that trains working into Wells station should be provided with a continuous brake and that more time should be allowed for the journey from Walsingham to Wells.[9]

An unusual incident occurred on the Great Eastern Railway when an engine driver and his fireman were convicted of stealing a box of silk valued at £70. The men were seen on a siding breaking into a Great Eastern truck, which contained the silk. They were also charged with stealing a box containing goods to the value of £10 belonging to the railway company. When the house of one of the prisoners was searched in order to recover the silk, the police found a box containing a silver mug, a silver cruet stand, four glasses, and six pairs of scissors, all of which belonged to the company. The box had been lost in transit from Sheffield. After a jury had found both men guilty, William Naylor, the engine driver, was sentenced to 11 months' imprisonment, and Charles Rawlins, the fireman, was sentenced to six months' imprisonment.[10]

In addition to the engine driver and fireman, each train carried a guard, who had wide-ranging responsibilities. Each guard was issued with a distinctive uniform with his designation and the initials of the company emblazoned on the collar. The guard was responsible for the safe arrival and departure of his train, and for assisting the driver in braking when the train was not fitted with a continuous brake. In an emergency, the guard was responsible for placing detonators on the track to warn following trains of danger ahead. The responsibilities of guards were clearly set out in the 1846 Eastern Counties Railway Regulations:

> "Previous to the train being started, the guard must see that the carriages are all properly coupled, that there are proper brakes in the train, that the tail, side, and roof-lamps are attached and lighted if required, and on the journey he will from time to time look to the tail and side lamps, and see that they continue lighted; that the luggage is properly placed and protected, and that the carriages are in a proper state of cleanliness. After the train is started it is entirely under the control of the guard; the passengers and luggage are in his charge, and he is responsible for the safety and regularity of the train."

Letters to newspapers suggest that the guard on early East Anglian railways was held in high esteem by the travelling public:

> "The guard is the traveller's attendant; at unexpected stoppages you look to him for information; his watch never goes fast or slow, at strange junctions and stations you inquire the length of the stay from him; he is your personal Bradshaw, and he looks after you as carefully as the parcels in his van. You do not recognise the full work of the guard till you think of it; you see him when the train comes into his possession, making a note of the number of the carriages; he ushers you to your seat, takes a fatherly interest in your belongings…"[11]

Guards were essential members of the train crew, and consequently they were required to work on both passenger and freight trains. They were able to assist in stopping the train by applying a brake in the guard's van, a practice that could be achieved by various whistles specially devised to enable the driver and guard to communicate. Freight trains often consisted of a large number of wagons, and it was the responsibility of the guard to assist in shunting operations as required. Shunting was a dangerous practice, and this was demonstrated at Broxbourne Junction on the Great Eastern Railway in 1863 when two guards who were engaged in shunting became careless in their work and were run over by the wagons. Both men were killed.[12] A guard on a passenger train was responsible for resolving any disputes between passengers, and for noting any defects in the carriages under his control. Smoking in carriages often caused trouble, so in 1846 the Eastern Counties put special 'Smoking Saloon' carriages into service.

> "The Eastern Counties 'Smoking Saloons' were six-wheeled carriages, 15ft long and 7ft high inside, fitted with tables and lighted by colza-oil lamps, entered from an open 5ft platform at each end. Compared with the normal compartments which were only 6ft long with 6ft headroom and unlighted, their luxury caused much discontent among the non-smoking users of the line."[13]

Throughout the 19th century there were instances of passengers being robbed or molested whilst travelling in railway compartments, and this led to various solutions being put forward to resolve the problem. The following method of communication was never put into general use:

> "The desirableness of establishing a communication between passengers and railway guards has given birth to many inventions, but we have seen none more simple than one by Mr J. Brown, a pattern maker. By pulling a silken cord which is within easy reach the alarmed traveller may force the lamp through the roof of the carriage, and elevate it sufficiently high to attract the attention of the guard."[14]

The early railway companies were strict employers, and any breach of their regulations was considered to be a serious matter. When, in 1846, a driver on the Eastern Counties Railway found that his engine could not cope with a fully loaded luggage train, he separated the train and left part of it on the main line. The Guard should have made arrangements to protect the train, either by placing detonators, or by ensuring that an adequate warning of danger was given to approaching engines; however, no action was taken, and consequently a collision took place. The driver, Thomas Blackburn, appeared before the Magistrates at Ilford to answer a charge brought by the Eastern Counties. After all the evidence had been heard the Magistrates found that the driver had been guilty of a dereliction of duty in not complying with the regulation. He was therefore fined £5. A number of drivers and firemen attended the hearing, and they obviously felt sympathy for Blackburn for they arranged a collection and paid the fine for him. He was then discharged.[15]

# 4

## FREIGHT

The railways brought to an end the era of the mail coach. Railways offered a faster and cheaper means of carrying goods, sufficient reasons for the Post Office to employ the early railway companies to carry mail. At first, mail coaches were loaded onto trucks and transported between towns. They were then offloaded on reaching their destinations and continued as horse-drawn vehicles. However, the railway network expanded rapidly, enabling the Post Office to transfer the distribution of all mail from coach to train, and consequently mail coach services ceased completely. Long distance carriers were also adversely affected by railways. When the Eastern Counties line was opened between Colchester and London, it severely affected the profitability of carriers as their trade rapidly diminished. Most of the long distance carriers eventually closed their businesses when it became apparent that railways would eventually serve most of East Anglia.[1] The transportation of East Anglian goods by rail commenced in earnest in November 1846, when the first goods train arrived at Bury St Edmunds carrying 24 tons of general goods and 900 tons of coal.[2] Goods traffic increased rapidly, and the following year a goods train arrived at Ipswich from Stowmarket hauling 149 loaded wagons.[3] The carrying of freight soon became a most profitable area of railway operations, and of particular importance was the carriage of perishable goods:

> "The relative high speed of the railways allowed perishables to be carried from the country to the large towns and by the late 1840s London was receiving over 70 tons of fresh fish a week from the ports of Yarmouth and Lowestoft courtesy of the Eastern Counties Railway."[4]

Passenger traffic initially provided the railway companies with more revenue than freight traffic, and by 1841 revenue from passengers was three times that provided by freight. However, although passenger traffic continued to increase rapidly, freight traffic grew at an even faster rate, and by 1852 the carriage of freight became the most profitable part of the railway companies' operations. At the end of the 19th century, freight revenue exceeded passenger revenue by between 20 and 25 per cent. Not until 1971 did passenger revenue regain the lead.[4A]

The larger East Anglian stations had a goods office that handled the dispatch and receipt of goods, and clerks were employed to carry out this work. Goods to be dispatched were entered in the 'outward goods book', with each entry in the following form – Name of Sender, Address, Description of Goods, and Weight. After the appropriate carriage charges had been determined, the goods were then sent to their destinations on goods trains. Goods arriving at a station were usually unloaded by porters and then placed in the goods office to await collection. The meticulous record-keeping required of railway clerks caused many to leave railway work in search of more favourable employment. In 1844/45 the rate of resignations for clerks alone on the Eastern Counties was approximately three per cent per annum.[5]

The early railway companies issued strict conditions for the carriage of goods. The following regulations were printed on all conveyance notes issued by the Eastern Union Railway:

> "They will not be accountable for any Article, unless it be entered and signed for as received by them or their agents. Nor will they be responsible for the loss of, or damage done to Money in Cash, or Bills, or Promissory Notes, or Securities for Money, or Jewellery, Trinkets, Rings, Precious Stones, Bullion, Gold and Silver, Plate, or Plated Articles, Clocks, Watches, Time-pieces, Lace, Furs, Silks, in a manufactured or unmanufactured state, and whether wrought up or not wrought up with other Materials; Writings, Title Deeds, Prints, Paintings, Maps Engravings, Pictures, Stamps, or other valuables; nor for damage done to China, Glass, Wearing Apparel, Musical Instruments, Furniture, Toys, or any other such hazardous or brittle Articles, in packages or otherwise, unless the same be insured according to their value, and paid for at the time of delivery.

Nor for the Loss or Damage of any Goods put into returned Wrappers or Boxes; nor for any Goods left until called for, or to order, or left, or warehoused for the convenience of the parties to whom they are consigned.

Nor for the Loss or Damage of any Packages, insufficiently or improperly packed, marked, directed, or described, or containing a variety of Articles, liable by breaking to damage each other; nor for Leakage, arising from bad Casks or Cooperage.

All Goods received for the purpose of being carried, will be considered as subject to a general Lien, and held for money due for the Carriage of such Goods, and also for the general Balance owing by the owners to the Eastern Union Railway Company. If in Fourteen days after Notice has been given, that such Goods are detained for the above purposes, the Money due be not paid, they will be sold by Auction.

No claim for loss or damage (for which the Eastern Union Railway Company hold themselves accountable), will be allowed unless made within three days of the delivery of the Goods. The delivery of Goods will be considered complete when the same are unloaded out of the Waggon, Dray, or Cart, and placed at the door of the Consignees; the Cellaring or Warehousing of them afterwards will be at the Owner's risk.

N.B. – The above Conditions apply to all Goods received by the Eastern Union Railway Company at their respective Offices and Warehouses, wheresoever situate."[6]

In February 1860 the outward goods book at Harleston station in Norfolk was produced at the trial of Horace Beaumont, a Labourer, who was accused of stealing a turkey from Flixton Hall. When Beaumont was recognised by an employee at Flixton Hall, enquiries were made at Harleston station, where a Porter confirmed that Beaumont had arranged for a hamper containing the turkey to be sent to Maidenhead in Berkshire. The hamper and turkey were subsequently recovered and sent back to Norfolk, and at the trial of Beaumont at Bungay Petty Sessions the outward goods book was produced to confirm that Beaumont was named as the sender of a hamper of weight 20lbs. The address to which the hamper was to be sent was also given, and it was also recorded that the hamper was sent by the 3.30pm goods train on the same afternoon. The Porter who had dealt with the matter was called to identify Beaumont, and in light of the evidence Beaumont received two months' hard labour.[7]

The services operated jointly by the Norfolk Railway and the Eastern Counties Railway were constantly subjected to criticism. Breakdowns and accidents were frequent, and the London terminus of the Eastern Counties Railway was said to be inefficient, because of its poor management of goods. A shortage of locomotives and poor timekeeping added to the general dissatisfaction.

> "The newspapers report several instances where trains were seriously late, causing for one example, farmers' consignments of animals to miss their market, and in another, fish wagons so delayed at Brandon that the merchants were claiming compensation."[8]

The transport of cattle was also problematical as the animals could leap out of the open trucks. Drovers travelling with their cattle were expected to purchase a ticket at full rate, or travel with the animals in the open trucks. An attempt to raise fares in 1846 and to impose more stringent conditions on travel caused farmers to revolt. They were particularly displeased to learn that "the rail carriage of cattle in eastern England was at approximately double the rate charged in Belgium."[9]

The dispatch of livestock to locations outside of London was usually accomplished successfully, but mistakes could sometimes occur. In 1862 a Dealer forwarded 100 pigs from Norwich to Lincolnshire by the Eastern Counties Railway. At the station the pigs were put into a bullock-van, and because it was raining a Porter covered the van with a tarpaulin. However, when the van arrived at Peterborough it was discovered that all but three of the pigs were dead, death having been caused by suffocation. Consequently, the animals, which were once meant for pork, had to be converted into manure. The amount of compensation paid by the railway company for this careless act by one of its porters was not recorded.[10]

The second half of the 19th century saw an increase in the amount of perishable goods sent by rail from East Anglia. The Fens produced fruit, vegetables, sugar beet and malting barley, and these goods, together with the addition of fish and farm products, could be dispatched to markets throughout Industrial England.[11] However, the Eastern Counties railway was limited by the number of wagons available for freight train working. Between 1856 and 1860 the total number of wagons available increased only slightly from 6,103 to 6,305, and even the number of locomotives available for this period was limited, increasing from 271 to only 292.[12] The Eastern Counties Railway was, however, more successful in the transportation of heavy freight, particularly when used to carry some enormous cast iron girders for use in bridge construction at Langford in Essex. These girders, cast in 1847, were some of the largest to have been manufactured in the mid-19th century, being 53ft 4½in in length, and weighing about 13 tons each. The girders were cast at a foundry in Derby and sent to Pickford's wharf in the City Road by water. They were then moved to Bishopsgate station on the Eastern Counties line and sent by rail to Witham Station. It took 18 horses to draw the first girder from the station to Langford by means of two specially constructed trucks. The girder had to be taken on a circuitous route via Hatfield Peverel because of its size, taking from Thursday to the following Tuesday to complete the journey. A shorter route along Maldon Road was adopted for transportation of the second girder.[13]

By the end of the 19th century, the Great Eastern Company had taken over the East Anglian railway network, and agricultural producers consistently complained that they were unable to get produce to market quickly and cheaply by rail. A solution was put forward by the railway company whereby boxes of choice agricultural produce could be sent by passenger trains at very low rates. The Farmers, however, remained unhappy about the charges for this service, and it was pointed out that:

> "A gentleman last week bought of a Farmer at Upminster, in Essex, a hundredweight of potatoes to be delivered at Croydon. The charge was 2s, 6d for the potatoes and 2s, 6d for the railway freight. The distance is 25 miles. A purchase made of another farmer at Ilford, which is 18 miles from Croydon, cost 2s, 6d for the potatoes, and 9d for the carriage – by road. Thus the railway is three times as dear as the old horse cartage, in at least some instances. The cost of bringing potatoes from New York to London by sea is 6d per cwt,

the distance being rather over 3,000 miles. Ships are worked at less cost than railways, but 500 times as cheaply is an astounding conclusion."[14]

The East Suffolk Railway, which opened in 1859, had branch lines for both the carriage of passengers and freight. These branch lines were constructed to serve Lowestoft, Aldeburgh, and Framlingham. A further branch line led from the main line to Snape, but this branch was used for freight working only. The working conditions at Snape station were most unusual, but no doubt most satisfactory for the staff that worked there. There was only one freight train per day for the nearby maltings, so:

> "Once wagons were loaded or sheeted or shunted into the maltings or prepared for the outward journey, and consignment notes and wagon labels completed, there was often very little to do, and in summer an occasional swim was taken in the River Alde or a few pints were supped with the locals in the Plough and Sail Public House. At one time a spare set of fishing rods was kept on hand so that the odd hour or two could be whiled away on the riverbank."[15]

Access to the North Sea allowed East Anglian ports to trade with other counties and foreign countries. The amalgamation of the Ipswich and Bury Railway with the Eastern Union Railway in 1847 generated goods traffic for Ipswich docks, and by the end of the 19th century the docks were flourishing with up to 1,000 coastal sailings a year and regular links with Sweden, Norway and the Black Sea.[16] The railways also operated freight services to King's Lynn, Wells, Lowestoft and Yarmouth, although the port at Wells gradually reduced in importance due to silting of the harbour. A branch line from Westerfield to Felixstowe Pier was opened for passengers and freight in 1877, allowing Felixstowe to develop into a major port, providing employment opportunities for dock workers and railwaymen. The Great Eastern Railway began operating a weekly cargo service from Harwich to Rotterdam in 1863, allowing foreign trade to flourish, and in 1886 docks were opened at Tilbury to deal with freight operations. Felixstowe, Harwich and Tilbury have subsequently developed into three of the most important ports in the UK.

# 5

## Signalling

In order to prevent collisions the early East Anglian Railways were operated on the 'time interval' system. Trains were released at intervals of ten minutes on the assumption that after ten minutes the line ahead would be clear. Although trains were few and far between in the early days, this system was clearly unsatisfactory. If the leading train was involved in an accident, or suffered a mechanical breakdown, the driver of the following train had no way of knowing that the line was blocked. However, on the Eastern Counties and Eastern Union railways, rudimentary signalling was provided by policemen who acted as signalmen and pointsmen. These policemen wore top hats, and gave hand signals to the train drivers to indicate 'all right', 'caution', and 'danger'. The 'all right' signal was given by extending the arm horizontally, whereas the 'caution' signal was given by holding one arm straight up, or by showing a green flag. A red flag was used for the 'danger' signal or "in the absence of a red flag, by holding both arms straight up, or waving with violence a hat or any other object."[1]

In addition to the hand signals given by policemen there were other fixed signals upon which lamps could be hung at night. Most of these signals were worked by the policeman who had to go to each signal to operate it. As passenger traffic increased, it became necessary to install semaphore signals and the Eastern Counties Company therefore placed an order with Messrs. Stevens & Co., of Darlington Works, Southwark Bridge Road, London, who manufactured this equipment.[2] The signals had three positions; horizontal meant 'stop', inclined downwards indicated 'caution', and dropped right down so that the arm fitted into a slot in the post and was out of sight showed 'line clear'. A red light was used for stop, green for caution and white for clear.[3]

There were frequent incidents of carelessness by policemen in the early days, which could have resulted in serious accidents. Hugh Moffat gives details of such carelessness in *East Anglia's First Railways*.

"The following incidents were reported to the directors of the Eastern Union Railway on one day in September 1846:

James Scrivener, policeman at Lawford, reported for not signalling special engine returning from Colchester – J S fined one week's wages.

Constables Andrews and Tunmer reported for not giving the proper signal to a driver approaching Belstead Cutting on the 14th, when the rails were being lifted. They were called in and the Board having heard extenuating circumstances, it was ordered that Andrews and Tunmer be reprimanded by the Chairman, which was accordingly done.

Switchman Cole having been reported asleep in his box on Sunday evening last upon the arrival of the Down Mail and not being in attendance as he had been ordered."[4]

In addition to acting as signalmen and pointsmen, railway police were also employed to patrol stations, yards, and outbuildings on the line, and this often led to arrests being made. On 24th March 1866 at 4.30am on a Sunday morning, Sergeant Frederick Standingford of the Great Eastern Railway police, stationed at Wymondham, apprehended James Clarke near to the railway station. Clarke, who was an off-duty fireman with the railway company, was putting rolls of cloth into an empty truck. However, when he saw the policeman approach he dropped the cloth and ran off along the Dereham railway line, pursued by Standingford. Clarke then turned and threw stones at the policeman, but eventually he was overpowered and with the assistance of Hunt, the night porter, was taken to the railway station. He then offered the policeman a sovereign for his release, which was declined, so turning his attention to Hunt he offered him £5, which was also declined. He was subsequently handed over to the Norfolk police and was found to be carrying skeleton keys and a chisel. The cloth had been sent from Huddersfield, consigned to Mr Bates of Dereham, and Clarke had stolen the cloth from a truck which had been left between Ely and Wymondham.[5]

Following a working agreement between the Norfolk Railway

Company and the Eastern Counties Company in 1846 the electric telegraph was adopted for use throughout the system.

> "It was also agreed to instruct the Electric Telegraph Company to provide five wires along the lines from London to Brandon, from which latter place the Norfolk Company were to have a similar number provided to carry the connection through from London to Norwich and Yarmouth.
>
> The public use of the telegraph at this time was not as general as it is today, no doubt accounted for by the minimum charges, some of which are given:
>
> | | |
> |---|---|
> | London to Stratford, Ilford, Romford, Brentwood, Tottenham, or Broxbourne | 2s 0d |
> | London to Colchester, Bishop's Stortford, or Cambridge | 3s 6d |
> | London to Ely or Brandon | 5s 0d |
> | London to Norwich | 7s 6d |
> | London to Yarmouth | 9s 6d"[6] |

The introduction of the electric telegraph coincided with the semaphore signals being operated by levers, which could also operate the points. These levers were grouped together in signal boxes, and the telegraph enabled signalmen in these boxes to communicate with each other. The 'time interval' system was now superseded by the 'block system', whereby trains were separated by space, so that no two trains were allowed to be in the same 'section'. Each line was divided into sections, and before a signalman allowed a train to enter any section he had first to ascertain that the train in front had cleared it at the other end.[7] There were a number of single lines in East Anglia, so in order to prevent collisions the Great Eastern Railway adopted the train staff and ticket system. The first single line to use this method of working was the Waveney Valley branch in 1864.[8] A driver was given a baton, either of wood or metal, at the beginning of each section, and this was carried on the engine until the end of the section was reached. The baton was then made available to the driver of the next train to return along the line. However, sometimes it became necessary for two trains to travel in a section at the same time, one closely following the other. After inspecting the baton at the start of the journey the driver of the first train was given a ticket, and the baton was then carried by the driver of the second train. A ticket could only be issued to a driver after an inspection of the baton had been carried out.

Before the introduction of the train staff and ticket system the safe operation of single lines depended upon engine drivers correctly reading semaphore signals. On 10th September 1864 an accident occurred on the section of line between Beccles station and the swing bridge over the River Waveney. A goods train left Beccles station at 7.30pm on a very dark night, and because the driver had not paid proper attention to the signals the goods train was met by a fish train from Yarmouth. However, neither driver was aware of the danger because of the limited visibility. The collision that subsequently occurred damaged both engines and wrecked many of the trucks being hauled by the goods train. The drivers and their Firemen, although badly injured, all survived the accident.[9]

Working as a signalman was a stressful occupation. The job carried enormous responsibility, as all signalmen worked long hours, and although working in a signal box was relatively safe compared to other jobs on the railways, accidents could occur, as shown by the following serious accident that occurred at Chappel railway station in 1865:

## "FATAL ACCIDENT AT CHAPPEL RAILWAY STATION

An inquest was held at the Railway Hotel, Chappel on Wednesday last before W. Codd Esq. Coroner, on the body of Ephraim Stone, signalman at the above Station.

James Shadwell said: I was the guard of the 8.30pm goods train for Sudbury and Marks Tey, and on the arrival of my train I told the signalman he had one truck off for Halstead line. I went up into the signal box to ask Stone for a book I had lent him, as soon as the truck was let into the siding. Stone came down the steps and I followed him, but Stone was used to the steps, and came down faster than I could. He had his lamp in his hand and went in front of the truck. He looked towards it before he went across. I saw his lamp fly up and immediately the truck jumped up and I saw by my lamp the two hind wheels pass over him. I thought he was going to scotch it up to prevent it going too far up the siding.

He said he was coming down when I first went up the steps to him; that he would come down and lend me a hand. After I saw the truck go over him I went to him and lifted up his head and said 'Mate are you hurt?' but he did not speak and was no doubt dead."[10]

Despite working long hours signalmen were often expected to attend religious gatherings. Bible classes were held at Lowestoft station on Sunday mornings and afternoons, and these were attended by porters, signalmen and others. It was said that these classes, and other efforts made for their spiritual good, were much appreciated by the men themselves. Sometimes the men were rewarded for attendance:

"Through the kindness of the promoters, an excellent tea was given to them at the St John's District Hall, kindly lent for the occasion by the Rev. T. C. Chapman, the esteemed vicar, who presided. There were about 70 present, including the wives of the men, and during the evening addresses were delivered by the Chairman, the Rev. S. B. Driver, Mr Chas. Dobbin (of the great Eastern Railway Company), besides several of the men."[11]

In 1872 the Great Eastern Railway Company settled a long running pay dispute by increasing the wages of engine drivers, firemen, and signalmen by about two shillings a week. However, the signalmen claimed that they should have additional pay for working on Sundays, and for the long hours worked. The Company eventually accepted this argument, but at the half-yearly meeting of the Great Eastern Railway in 1875 it was noted that the rise in wages for signalmen and the reduction of their hours of duty had considerably affected operational costs.[12] However, despite this settlement, low pay and long hours remained, and were grudgingly accepted as part of signal box work, but by the end of the 19th century it became apparent that overworked signalmen were responsible for a number of serious railway accidents. *The Graphic* newspaper published the following article about the situation in 1890:

"As the recent railway disasters at Taunton and Chalk Farm were both due to the default of signalmen it is of vital importance to the public apart from any philanthropic impulses – that these officials should be thoroughly fit for their responsible and exacting duties. People may wonder why Rice – the poor fellow whose lapse of memory caused the disaster at Norton Fitzwarren – had not retired from his post, seeing that he was 64 years of age, and had not long before received an injury to his head – but the simple reason probably is that he could not afford it, and therefore, like other elderly men in similar circumstances, clung on until he should be actually ordered to go. Some light is thrown on this subject by a statement made at the Railway Employees Congress by Mr James Bedford, the President. We hope it may be exaggerated but we fear there is a large substratum of truth in it… Mr Bedford says – "Signalmen in some of the country districts are worked 15, 16, 18, and even 20 hours per day for a miserable wage of from 14s to 22s per week. Men of from 65 to 70 were still working in signal boxes because if they resigned their only place was the workhouse, as the companies would not grant them their justly earned pensions." Lord Norton, again, who can speak with some authority on this subject, and who is not likely to overstate his case, points out that there are now only two relays of signalmen in the 24 hours, instead of three, as formerly, and that 12 continuous hours of such work, requiring incessant attention, is more than an average man can stand. He also maintains that, besides shorter hours, there should be an assistant in every signal box. These reforms will, of course, cost the shareholders money, but they ought not to grudge it, and, in the long run they may find it may save them some of the large sums which they now pay by way of compensation for accidents. If, however, they refuse to do it voluntarily, Parliament should compel them to be more generous."[13]

The adverse working conditions did not seem to deter men from East Anglian signal box work, and working careers of 40 years or more were not uncommon. Mr A. S. Lack retired in September 1913 after 42 years' service with the Great Eastern Railway. He joined as a porter at Yarmouth (Vauxhall) and was subsequently appointed signalman at Whitlingham in December 1874. He then transferred to Norwich (Thorpe) signal box in January 1876, where he remained until his retirement.[14]

The head signalmen at the west box at Liverpool Street were both in post for lengthy periods. Mr Charles Morgan passed the whole of his service of 37 years in the west box, retiring in April 1913. He served under five Superintendents and seven Station Masters, and he saw his box enlarged from 100 to 244 levers. His friend and colleague, Mr Frederick Neale, who worked with Mr Morgan on the same shift for 31 years, retired in November 1910 after 46 years' service. He joined the Great Eastern Railway at Stratford in 1864.[15]

# 6

## Platelayers

In 1844 the first purchase of rails for the new Eastern Union Railway was given to a Shropshire company at an initial cost of £6 15s per ton, but by 1845, when further rails were purchased, the cost had risen to £9 10s per ton. Tenders were also invited for sleepers, and it was specified that they should be made from larch, oak, or fir. The sleepers used on the construction of the Eastern Union Railway were priced at 6s 6d each, and these were imported from Scandinavia and the Baltic. Chairs were required to hold the rails in place, and these were obtained from the Ipswich firm of Ransomes & May, which also supplied the wooden pegs or 'treenails' that were used to secure the chairs to the sleepers.[1]

Once constructed, the permanent way required regular maintenance, and initially inspection work was carried out by railway policemen. However, as the railways developed, additions were made to the permanent way so that the term included telegraph posts, gradient boards, 'whistle' boards, and mile and quarter mile posts. There were also water columns, coal stages, and pits between the rails to allow drivers to get under engines for examination.[2]

The work required to maintain this expanded permanent way necessitated the employment of gangs of operatives who became known as platelayers. The platelayers were supervised by a superintendent or inspector who was responsible for:

> "… the efficient state of the way committed to their care, and the protection of the Company's premises and property belonging thereto, for which purpose they will be made special constables; thus being authorised to arrest any person or persons trespassing or damaging the works, taking the party so offending to the nearest station, to be dealt with as the law directs."[3]

Each foreman platelayer was issued with a set of tools consisting of "one level, three beaters, two bars, one lever, two hammers, one gauge, one mill, one set of heights, one auger, and a truck."[4]

In order to signal engine drivers to stop, platelayers were also issued with a red flag, a green flag, and a lantern for use at night. The signal to the engine driver had to be given 600 yards in advance of any obstruction, and if a flag were to be mislaid the platelayer was instructed to wave a handkerchief. At night, a red light was shown to stop a train, and a green light was used if a reduction in speed was required.[5]

Working on railway lines was a dangerous occupation, and extreme care had to be taken in order to prevent serious accidents. In September 1850 nine platelayers were killed whilst working on the Eastern Counties Railway. The *Ipswich Journal* reported the accident as follows:

> "At eight o'clock in the morning a number of men were engaged in new ballasting the line, and were at work near the bridge, just beyond the Brentwood station. Having just discharged a quantity of gravel between the rails, they jumped from the waggons and commenced spreading it over the ground, and while so engaged the early train from Colchester approached the spot. Unhappily, in consequence of the dense fog at the time and the noise of the engine of the ballast trucks blowing off its steam, the approach of the up-train was unheeded until it was within 50 yards of the workmen. The foreman of the gang cried out to the men, who, by some strange fatality, stepped on the up-line instead of on the middle space. The engine passed over nine of them, causing instant death in every case, and mutilating the bodies in a frightful manner."[6]

In addition to giving warning signals to engine drivers, platelayers were responsible for making sure that rails on the main line and at switch points and crossing points were set at the correct gauge. The Eastern Counties Railway initially set the gauge at 5ft, but in 1844 the gauge on the lines from London to Chelmsford and Cambridge was altered to 4ft 8½ inches to enable connections to be made to other railways.[7] The duty of each platelayer was set out in the regulations as follows:

"To maintain the rails in proper gauge, perfect in line and level, and safe in all other respects. To scrape, and sweep the rails, so as to keep them clean, and free from dirt and snow during the winter season. To examine the whole of his length every morning before train time, and to see that it is in a safe state for their passage; the neglect of this precaution will subject the platelayer to a heavy penalty, or immediate dismissal. To remove all loose stones, iron, or other materials from the road, and to keep the line clear from interruption of any kind."[8]

The regular examination of sleepers, fishplates and chairs was essential in order to make sure that the rails were secure. It was found that the wooden treenails that fixed the chairs to the sleepers often worked loose as the weight of trains became heavier, and this could lead to derailments. Therefore by 1850 treenails had been replaced by iron fastenings, and the chairs themselves had been redesigned.[9] Regulations could not, however, prevent acts of carelessness. On 1st September 1905 the 9.27am express train from Liverpool Street to Cromer approached Witham Station on the Great Eastern Railway at a speed of nearly 70 miles per hour. Both the driver and his fireman noted that there were three platelayers working on the line, who only stepped away from the crossover work on which they were engaged at the last moment. The engine and its tender cleared the crossover, but the remaining 14 carriages of the train became derailed. This resulted in a fire breaking out in a first class carriage due to leaking gas, whilst another carriage was thrown onto the platform, demolishing the porter's and ticket collector's room, and killing the single occupant. One carriage overturned and was smashed to pieces, killing all eight occupants. The three platelayers, Arthur Newman, Morris Pavelin, and Foreman Platelayer Robert Pryke, when questioned about the accident, stated that they were only clearing ballast from the 'V' of the crossing, but they denied loosening any of the rails. The initial inquiry was abandoned, but a second hearing took place when a witness came forward to state that he saw the train pass over the points and then saw one of the rails fly into the air. The train driver also noted that as he passed the three platelayers their eyes were fixed on the crossover. It became apparent that the platelayers had loosened the rail fastening at the 'V' of the crossover, and did not have time to tighten it before the train arrived. They had also failed to use a red flag to warn the train driver that work was being carried out on the line.[10]

Royal trains frequently crossed East Anglia, and when these trains were scheduled, strict instructions were issued to railway staff.

> "Drivers must see that their engines are not emitting smoke or steam or whistling while the Royal train is passing; and drivers of passenger trains passing the Royal train must avoid whistling unless it is absolutely necessary, and must also shut off steam while running past."[11]

Platelayers had specific duties on these occasions.

> "It is a special instruction to station-masters to arrange for the placing of trustworthy men at 'facing points' over which the Royal train will run, half an hour before the train is due. These 'facing points' must also be carefully examined, and bolted and padlocked for the line on which the Royal special is travelling. No work which is likely to affect the line must go on at any of the stations and all work in connection with the permanent way must cease a quarter of an hour before the train is due… In addition it is the station-masters' duty to see that the entrances to their stations are watched and kept private. All fogmen, whether there be any sign of fog or not, must be at their posts an hour before the Royal train is due."[12]

In the days of the Eastern Counties Railway, platelayers were given the concession of being able to cultivate spare land on the sides of the railway. The relevant regulation stated that "As an encouragement to industrious platelayers and labourers, they will have the free use of any spare land on the sides of the railway for growing vegetables, but they are not to cultivate more than they are able to manage before or after working hours; any platelayer working other than on the railway, during working hours, will be instantly dismissed."[13]

There were few other advantages of being employed on permanent way work. It was possible to progress from labourer to platelayer to ganger, and then to sub-inspector and inspector, and there was a clear wage differential between each grade. However, there was little opportunity to rise above these grades, and consequently these railway workers rarely went into other posts such as gatemen or signalmen.[14] In view of the fact that permanent way work was hard, with long hours spent outside, whatever the weather, a high turnover of staff should have been expected. However, some railwaymen spent their entire working lives on permanent way maintenance. Mr G. Jennings, platelayer of Trimley, who retired on the pension fund in November 1913, aged 66, joined the service as platelayer at Felixstowe Beach in May 1877. After 20 years there he was transferred to Trimley where he remained till his retirement.[15]

The rates of pay for permanent way work were relatively low compared to other railway jobs. The daily rates paid to the various grades in the 19th century are given in *Victorian Railwaymen* as follows:

|  | Average s d | Range s d s d |
|---|---|---|
| Gangers |  |  |
| 1840s | 4  5 | 4  0 – 5  0 |
| 1850s | 3  11 | 3  0 – 4  6 |
| Early 1870s | 3  8 | 3  6 – 5  0 |
| Platelayers |  |  |
| 1830s | 2  11 | 2  10 – 3  0 |
| 1840s | 3  2 | 3  0 – 3  6 |
| Labourers |  |  |
| 1830s | 2  5 | 2  3 – 2  6 |
| 1840s | 2  7 | 2  6 – 3  6 |
| Early 1870s | 2  10 | 2  6 – 3  6 |

The gangers' wages seem to have fallen, whereas the labourers' have risen slightly.[16] These rates were paid for working a seven-day week, with weekly hours ranging between 56 and 72 hours. On the Eastern Counties Railway the men were paid weekly, and were expected to give two weeks' notice before leaving. They were warned that all pay due would be forfeited if they failed to comply with this rule.[17] Any breach of the regulations invariably led to a fine, whilst being intoxicated at work resulted in instant dismissal. Towards the end of the 19th century all grades of staff on the Great Eastern Railway were closely monitored to guard against the unnecessary employment of staff. The following memorandum was sent from the District Superintendent's Office at Cambridge station to the unfortunate Station Master at Long Stanton station:

> "Dear Sir,
>
> <u>Extra Assistance</u>
>
> Why are you keeping an extra man on seeing you have a decrease of 134 tons and £284 also a decrease on your cattle traffic for last month.
>
> You had better pay the man off at once. I shall refuse to certify any more vouchers.
>
> Let me have your explanation and acknowledgement.
>
> Yours truly."[18]

Although platelayers maintained the permanent way in a safe condition, they were unable to prevent small children from playing on the rails. In 1851, over a period of several months, it was noted that objects were being deliberately placed on the Eastern Counties branch line between Maldon and Witham. These obstructions nearly led to a train from Maldon being derailed at a level crossing called Hutley's Crossing, about a mile from Witham station. The obstruction caused the engine to jump, but fortunately it remained on the line. When a police investigation was carried out, two little boys aged about ten were apprehended. Walter Smith and Christopher Courtman subsequently appeared in court where they admitted placing stones on the railway line. They were placed on remand for a period of one week. The police also apprehended Joseph Appleton, a 19-year-old, who admitted committing a similar offence about a month earlier. Appleton denied putting the stones on the rail, but said that he might have kicked one on. He was also remanded to enable the police to carry out further enquiries.[19]

In 1871 platelayers were responsible for the rescue of a child who had fallen from a train. The child, an eight-year-old boy, was booked from Cambridge to East Dereham on the Great Eastern line. He was placed in an unoccupied compartment by the guard, but during the course of the journey he unfastened the door and fell out, landing upon some grass growing by the side of the line. The incident occurred near Waterbeach, and fortunately there were some platelayers working nearby. The platelayers put the child on a trolley and took him to Waterbeach. He was then taken to hospital in Cambridge where it was found that he had broken his collar bone.[20]

# 7

# Hotels and Seaside Holidays

The early coaching inns provided food and overnight accommodation for those who wished to travel long distances by stagecoach, and the railway companies were quick to realise the financial advantage to be gained from providing similar services for their passengers. A major difficulty was in gaining approval for railway lines to locations that would be frequented by travellers. Approval for the construction of the line to Harwich proved to be particularly difficult, for in 1845 the Board of Trade announced that the last date for the reception of railway plans would be 30th November, and when the door at the Board of Trade was eventually closed at midnight no application had been received for a railway line to Harwich. The *Illustrated London News*, however, had a reporter waiting outside the premises and was able to report the following incident:

> "At the Board of Trade there were scenes of wild confusion as more and more last-minute arrivals drove up on that Sunday evening. The door was eventually closed at midnight: a quarter of an hour later a post-chaise which had got lost on the way drove up in hot haste with reeking horses. Its occupants (from Harwich) rang the doorbell, were refused admission, and so threw their vast roll of plans in through the open doorway, knocking the lamp over and breaking it. The plans were thrown out into the street again. When the door was opened a second time, the process was repeated (apart from the lamp), and at 2am, when the reporter left, the railway promoters from Harwich were still trying to gain admission."[1]

The promoters must have ultimately been successful, for shipping lines serving Rotterdam and Antwerp from Harwich were established in 1863 and 1864, and in 1865 a hotel was opened at the Quay in Harwich by the

Great Eastern Railway.[2]

By the end of the 19th century the Great Eastern Railway owned three hotels, which they promoted as 'Hotels by the Sea'. In addition to the Quay at Harwich, a further hotel had been opened at Parkeston Quay, and the Sandringham Hotel at Hunstanton was opened in 1876. In 1884 the Great Eastern Railway opened the fourth and largest of their hotels at Liverpool Street, and this proved to be the only hotel profitable for the railway company. A 1912 brochure described the advantages gained by travelling to the seaside as follows:

> "The Great Eastern Railway Company offer their patrons and the public, who may wish to spend a day or two away from the turmoil of busy town life, facilities which no other line can excel, since a few hours' ride from Liverpool Street will take visitors to any of the favourite and health-giving seaside resorts on the East Coast, which alone can restore exhausted nature to the elasticity and vigour which these days of telephones, telegraph and electricity demand."[3]

The advantages to be gained from a seaside visit were first recognised in the 18th century when "Medical opinion at the time began to expound the therapeutic virtues of sea air, and of both bathing in and drinking seawater – taking the seaside 'cure'."[4] The seaside resorts in East Anglia, being mostly located at considerable distances from London, did not develop until the coming of the railways. Early 19th century Cromer in Norfolk was initially a small fishing port, whilst Clacton in Essex was a small village. However, the availability of fast rail travel and cheap fares, coupled with the recognition by the railways that profits could be made, brought about a rapid increase in tourism. During the 19th century, railway lines were constructed to serve the East Anglia resorts of Cromer, Yarmouth, Lowestoft, Felixstowe, Clacton, and Southend, and consequently these resorts grew in size to accommodate the influx of tourists who arrived by railway on day excursions, works outings, or for longer holiday visits.

*The Graphic* newspaper considered Yarmouth and Lowestoft to be particularly favourable locations for a holiday visit, and gave a lengthy description of the delights that awaited the visitor to Yarmouth.

## "SKETCHES AT GREAT YARMOUTH.

"The sea coast of East Anglia is wanting in some of the attractions which characterise the shores of the western, and south-western counties. There are neither beetling precipices nor picturesque piles of rocks, and the adjacent inland scenery is apt to be tame and treeless. Per contra, there is a bracing quality in the air which is lacking in the soft and relaxing West, there is generally a good honest sandy or shingly beach, and the bathing is excellent. Anxious mammas, with children fond of climbing, will not regret the absence of precipices, as there is less fear of accidents from falls. Add to this one special attraction of the east coast, namely, that if you are an early riser the sun leaps from an ocean-bed, and sheds his genial horizontal rays on you as you bathe, while in the evening his departing effulgence reddens the sails of all the vessels in sight, and renders the seaward prospect especially attractive.

Among the east-coast watering places Yarmouth and Lowestoft are the best known. Lowestoft is deemed the most genteel, but Yarmouth is decidedly the most amusing. The wide extent of sand that lies between the Wellington and Britannia piers is during the month of August completely dotted over with pleasure-seekers, who never need be in want of amusements. Itinerant vendors abound who will furnish them with cakes, apples, and sweetmeats; they can have their likenesses taken in ferrotype; they can listen to negro melodies or view performing dogs; or, lastly, they can, for the small sum of sixpence, embark on board one of the excellent sailing boats which abound on the beach and gain an hour's experience of 'life on the ocean wave'. At night the piers are the centre of attraction, as there is generally a good band playing on one or both of them. Then the old town of Yarmouth itself is a picturesque and popular place, with its network of alleys or "rows", very narrow but scrupulously clean. Altogether, there is a very Dutch aspect about Yarmouth and its neighbourhood, and a sail up the river Yare especially recalls the 'lowlands of Holland'."[5]

Southend, being the nearest seaside resort to London, catered for large numbers of day excursion visitors from London, and by the end of the 19th century it had become known as 'Whitechapel-on-Sea'.[6] The Great Eastern Railway Company was particularly busy with excursionists on Bank Holidays. On Easter Monday 1871 thousands travelled to Broxbourne and Rye House by the Great Eastern Railway, whilst crowds left Fenchurch Street for Southend.[7] The 1876 August Bank Holiday drew even greater numbers of travellers. The London, Tilbury, and Southend line had at 2pm carried 9,000 to Southend, 8,000 to Rosherville, and 11,000 to Gravesend. Southend became so crowded that it proved impossible to find beds in the town, and it therefore became necessary for the railway company to provide sleeping accommodation for 570 persons in its carriages at Southend station.[8] Inevitably, with such large numbers of visitors, it was not unusual for trouble to break out:

> "Among the most popular of summer resorts is Southend, the pleasant sea border, where in the short compass of a day's outing we can enjoy a sniff of the briny, a plunge into salt water, a row or a sail, unlimited shrimps for tea, and a selection of some of the biggest oysters in England. Southend may be said to be the favourite resort of the working class of holiday-makers at the eastern end of London; but what is to become of it and of them if the incursion of a band of so-called labourers, sixty or seventy strong, and mostly drunk, enter the shops, seize on the oysters, for which they refuse to pay, attack the tradesfolk, brutally assaulting several persons, and resisting every attempt to bring them to order in a place where the feeble police force, thinking that discretion is the better part of valour, decline to interfere till a fresh contingent of artillerymen and police from Shoeburyness come to their aid? So serious was the disturbance that a contingent of police came from a distance of nineteen miles; and only when the train was about to start to convey the band of ruffians back to London were two or three of the ringleaders arrested."[9]

It was also possible to visit East Anglian resorts by using the Great Northern Railway, which offered day excursions to Cromer and Yarmouth for a return fare of four shillings. The company advertised their excursion as 'The New and Picturesque Route to Poppyland by the GNR', and it was certainly a journey to remember: "the climb over the Wolds by Castle Bytham, the drop down to Bourne, the run across the level fenland by the tulip fields of Spalding, the stiff pull beyond South Lynn up to the heaths of Norfolk, and then the long undulating descent through Melton Constable and North Walsham to the sea."[10] It was the Great Eastern Railway, however, which primarily served East Anglia, and this company advertised a range of excursions in the press:

"GREAT EASTERN RAILWAY
SEASIDE
TWO MONTHS and FORTNIGHTLY RETURN TICKETS are now issued at Reduced Fares to YARMOUTH, Lowestoft, Aldborough, Harwich, Dovercourt, Walton-on-the-Naze, and Hunstanton.

Special Excursion Train to Harwich, Dovercourt, and Walton-on-the-Naze, every Sunday at 9.00 and every Monday at 8.30am calling at Stratford. Fares 7s 6d, 5s 6d, and 3s.

Special Excursion Train to Hunstanton every Monday at 7.30am, calling at Bethnal Green, Old Ford, and Stratford. Fare there and back 4s.

Excursions to Broxbourne and Rye House every Sunday at 10am and on Monday and Saturday at 9.15 and 10.15am, and 12.45 and 2.45pm.

Epping Forest – Excursion tickets are issued to Woodford, Buckhurst Hill, and Loughton every Sunday and Monday, by all Trains. Fares 2s 6d, 1s 6d, and 1s.

For further particulars see handbills and time books.
London June 1873
S. Swarbrick, General Manager"[11]

Excursions for walkers were also popular. Travellers were advised to consult the timetables of the Southend Railway and take a train to Stanford-le-Hope, a few miles beyond Tilbury. They were then advised that by taking an easy walk through the town of Horndon, and then across the fields to Langdon, they would reach a neat little inn which provided clean and homely accommodation. "He must be a poor walker who could not accomplish the journey from Stanford to Langdon and back again – some seven miles in all – and find a few hours to spare."[12] However, the most profitable excursions for the railway companies, and the most difficult to organise, were the works outings that took place annually for employees of various companies. In 1893 a works excursion by the Bass brewery required 15 trains from Burton-on-Trent and one from St Pancras to carry 8,000 passengers to Great Yarmouth. Those travelling on the excursion were issued with a 16-page programme in which the Traffic Manager gave the following advice:

> "Let me advise all to get substantial food and so be fitted for the fatigue of such a long day. Avoid messes and odds and ends, rather partaking of MEALS at proper hours as you do when at your ordinary employment."[13]

By the end of the 19th century the first bogie carriages had appeared on the Cromer expresses, and restaurant cars were put into service. These restaurant cars appeared on the North Country Continental Express, and on the expresses between London and Cromer and Yarmouth.[14] The North Country Continental Express was one of the first cross-country services of its kind, running via Ipswich, Bury, and March, and it was unique in admitting third-class passengers to its dining car.[15] The reputation of the Great Eastern Railway was enhanced by these restaurant cars as the standard of service was notably high. The reputation of the company was further enhanced by its continental steamer services. For the 1881 Easter holiday, the press reported that "The Great Eastern Company arranged for two of their finest steamers to leave Harwich on Thursday night, the Lady Tyler for Rotterdam, and the Claud Hamilton for Antwerp. The boat Express will leave Liverpool Street station at 7.10pm, as usual, on Good Friday."[16] Luxurious ships and fast rail services attracted passengers, and by 1897 the Great Eastern Railway was able to convey 130,000 passengers on its vessels.[17] Continental services had certainly moved forward at great speed since the first disastrous excursion to a foreign port, which was organised by the Eastern Counties Railway in 1846:

> "On the return from Rotterdam, the crew of the steamer were drunk, a gale blew the ship off course and on the journey back to London the locomotive's boiler burst near Ely."[18]

In June 1904 the *Railway Magazine* gave details of a new and improved service for travellers using the Harwich-Hook of Holland route to the continent.

> "The Great Eastern Railway has placed a new and improved type of train on the service between Liverpool Street and Harwich (Parkeston Quay). The train has been constructed some six inches wider than other main line trains, is corridor throughout, and is suitably equipped with lavatory accommodation. Restaurant and breakfast cars are provided, so that passengers who have not time to dine in town can order refreshments a la carte on the down journey and it will be possible on the return journey to England to partake of table d'hote breakfast while travelling from the Essex coast to London. The train is lighted throughout by electricity, and provided for the winter months, with a system of heating which can be regulated in each carriage The lighting is by Stone's separate dynamo system, the dynamos being driven from the carriage axles. In the Great Eastern Railway Bill, which has passed through the House of Commons, powers are taken to run steam vessels between Harwich and the Hook of Holland, without proceeding to or starting from Rotterdam, and also to run steamers between Harwich and Zeebrugge."[19]

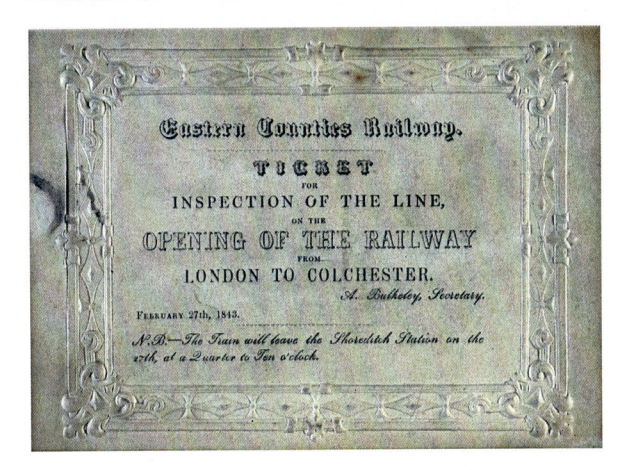

**Top left:** Former mistley signal box now at East Anglian Railway Museum
**Top right:** Two Eastern Counties Railway 2-2-2 locomotives outside Stratford Roundhouse © NRM Pictorial Collection /Science & Society Picture Libr
**Middle:** Workmen arriving at Liverpool Street © National Railway Museum / Science & Society Picture Libr
**Bottom:** Eastern Counties Railway inspection ticket, 1843 © National Railway Museum /Science & Society Picture Libr

***Top left:*** *Broad gauge locomotive, c.1890 © National Railway Museum / Science & Society Picture Libr*
***Top right:*** *Flooding at Stratford East station*
***Middle:*** *The dangerous Level Crossing at Barking*
***Bottom:*** *Shoreditch station – London terminus for Eastern Counties trains*

***Top left***: GER bus on Shotley route
***Top right:*** Chatteris Cambs interior of station signal box – early 1960s. Mr Bill Thorne (in photo) was the last signalman when the line closed (demolished 1964). Shows old Victorian equipment in detail
***Middle left:*** Chatteris Cambs railway station ticket booking office – early 1960s (demolished 1964 – bypass runs through site) Edmonson tickets on display
***Middle right:*** Great Eastern Railway train – Colchester station
***Bottom:*** Eastern Counties four wheel first class carriage

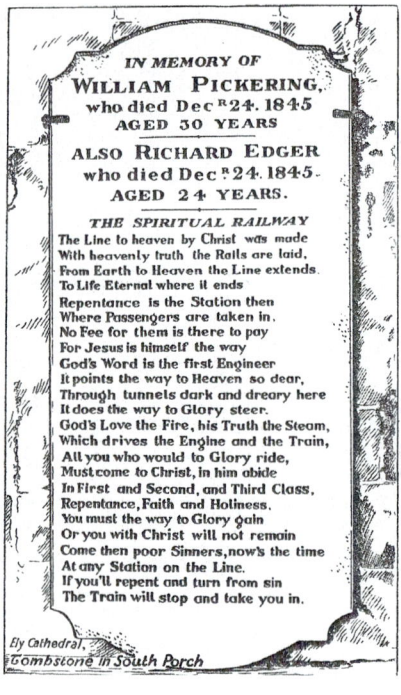

**Top:** *Arrival of Christmas Train at Shoreditch, 1849 (Eastern Counties Railway)*
**Left:** *Plaque to railwaymen on wall of Ely Cathedral*
**Middle right:** *Enfield Town station, c.1872*
**Bottom right:** *Great Eastern Railway, Frinton & Clacton Dining Car Express*

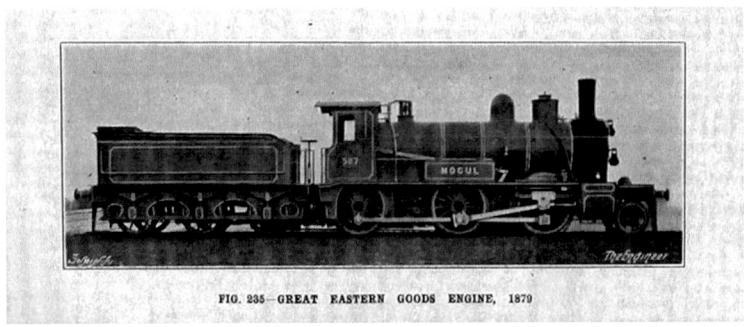

**Top:** *Great Eastern Railway loco Albert Dock at Gallions station*
**Middle:** *Great Eastern Railway goods engine – 1879*
**Bottom:** *Great Eastern Railway Express passenger engine – 1864*

*Top:* Great Eastern Railway engine No.1012, c.1910
*Middle left:* 1907 advertisement for East Anglian coastal resorts
*Right:* Great Eastern Railway porter W. Kidd – who retired as a driver at Stratford in 1920
*Bottom left:* Holden tank locomotive No.87, built at Stratford Works

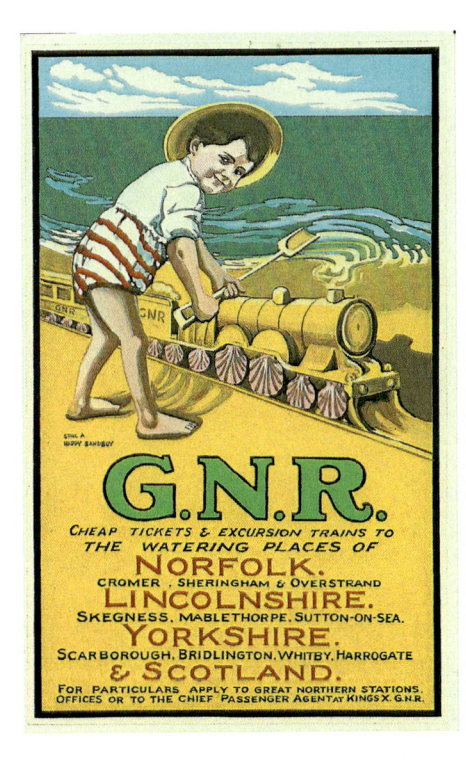

*Top:* Poster advertising the GER hotels available
*Left:* Great Northern Railway postcard advertising excursions to Norfolk
*Right:* Great Eastern Railway guard in full uniform

**Top left:** *Homersfield station – flood damage to track*
**Middle left:** *GER Hook of Holland express, c.1905*
**Bottom:** *Liverpool Street station – staircase leading to concourse*

*Top:* Great Eastern railway dining room at the Liverpool Street Hotel – c.1910
*Middle:* GER rolling stock and Holden engine in blue livery at Liverpool Street station
*Bottom:* Maldon East Station

***Top:*** *Melton signal box and Melton station staff - the horse was used for shunting*
***Middle:*** *Navvies at work on the railway track near Ipswich station*
***Bottom:*** *Platelayers at work*

**Top:** *Wolferton station used by royalty for Sandringham*
**Middle:** *GER 2-4-0 No.761 – used for the wedding of King George V, 6th July 1893*
**Bottom:** *A J15 engine – an engine of this type suffered a boiler explosion at Westerfield*

***Top:*** *Early semaphore signal*
***Middle:*** *Great Eastern Railway Saxby semaphore signals at Stratford West*
***Bottom:*** *Smoking carriage*

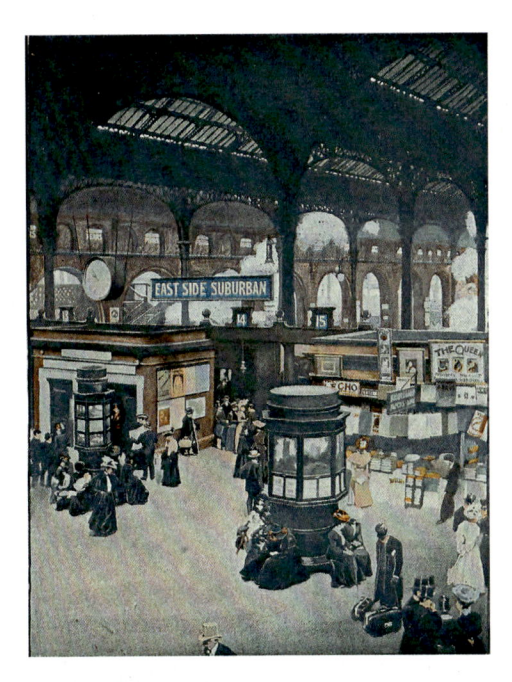

***Top:*** *Liverpool Street station – bookstall on eastern concourse*
***Middle:*** *Great Eastern Railway Southend train near Brentwood*
***Bottom:*** *GER 0-6-0 No.978 at Stratford works*

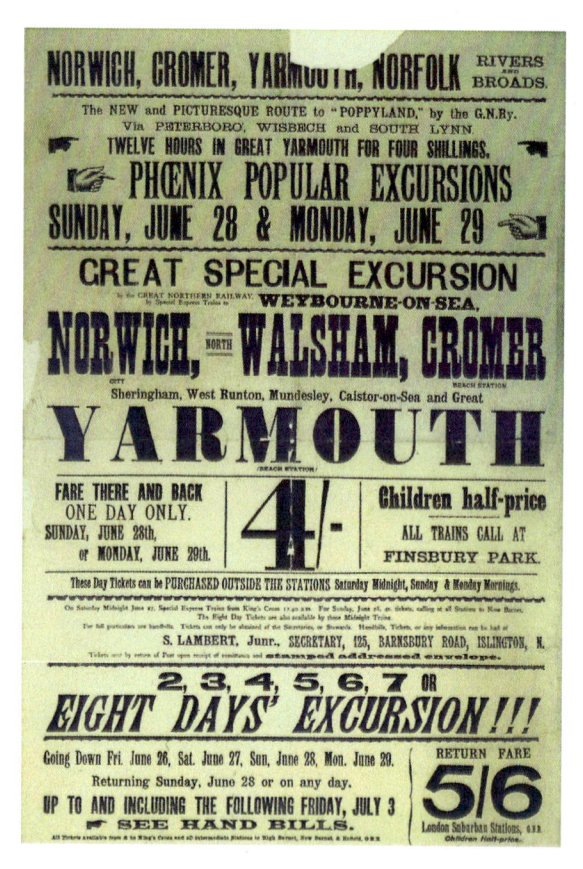

*Top:* Great Northern Railway excursion advertisement
*Bottom:* Damage to Wells station after engine ran through buffers

*These three photos are of the Westfield boiler explosion in 1900*

FIG. 79—TANK ENGINE, EASTERN COUNTIES RAILWAY, 1851

*Top:* Wilby station
*Middle:* Wreck of the Cromer express
*Bottom:* Tank engine, Eastern Counties Railway, 1851

# 8

## Accidents

Railway travel in the 19th century was a particularly unsafe form of transportation. Accidents were frequent, often resulting in the deaths of both passengers and railway employees. Railway workers were considered to be more exposed to risk than any other workers, due to overwork and long working hours. Very often, carelessness increased the risk of accidents, but safety was not a priority as the railway companies were not required by law to report accidents, and consequently they tended to be indifferent to the risks faced by their employees. The situation was improved in 1871 when the railway companies were required to inform the Board of Trade of every case of death or injury of railway workers.[1]

In 1862 the *Penny Illustrated Paper* published the accident statistics for railways for the year 1861:

> "RAILWAY ACCIDENTS – In railway annals every year might be distinguished by its special accidents. 1861 was the year of the Clayton Tunnel and the Kentish–town collisions, in which 38 passengers lost their lives and 498 were injured. In that year 284 persons were killed on railways in the United Kingdom. Forty-six of these passengers lost their lives from causes wholly beyond their own control, 38 by the two most calamitous collisions between trains, four by trains getting off the rails, and four by breakage of axles, wheels, &c, or by their getting out of order. It ought to be a warning that 18 passengers were killed last year through getting out of, or attempting to get into, trains in motion; 17 persons were killed while crossing at level crossings; 54 trespassers lost their lives, and 128 servants of companies or contractors. A passenger was killed at a station by leaning against a carriage to speak to another passenger, and falling in consequence of the train moving on. In the last five years

252 passengers have been killed by railway accidents, 132 of them from causes beyond their own control. 2,089 passengers have been injured also from causes beyond their own control; but the passengers must have been 750,000,000, perhaps more."[2]

In 1865 the Railway Benevolent Institution published a report on the situation, which stated that "Railway Servants have been shown to be liable to sickness, injuries and accidental death much beyond the average ratio: to diminish the causes of these to the utmost extent is a clear duty of the employers. Granted that they fulfil it as far as is in their power, the result still shows the unmistakeably hazardous nature of the employment."[3] However, improvements in rail safety were slow to occur, and railway accidents continued to occur throughout the 19th century.

The first railway to be constructed in East Anglia was the Eastern Counties railway. The appalling condition of the permanent way owned by this company should have led to serious accidents; however, in 1851 it was noted that no fatalities had occurred on its lines since 1846.[4] However, in 1856 the Board of Trade commissioned a report into the condition of the permanent way and its defective timber structures, and received assurances from the Eastern Counties Railway that remedial work would be undertaken where necessary.[5] The Eastern Union railway had a similarly good record with regard to fatalities caused by accidents, although at the opening of the Marks Tey to Sudbury line in July 1849 a minor incident occurred. The train carrying the Directors who had attended the opening ceremony collided with a floral arch when leaving Marks Tey, and the laurels and other decorations on the arch were carried off strung around the chimney and dome of the engine.[6] The precarious nature of railway work was, however, demonstrated in 1846 when:

"On Saturday last as John Kent, a Porter in the goods department at the Eastern Union station, was in the act of coupling the engine to an empty train, he inadvertently dropped his hand from the block onto the buffer rod whilst the engine was backing in, and crushed it in a frightful manner. Amputation was resorted to within half an hour. We are glad to hear that Kent is going on well."[7]

Because of the risks associated with railway travel, several insurance companies began to issue temporary insurance cover for railway journeys. Charles Dickens, writing in *Household Words*, was extremely enthusiastic about this practice:

> "You proceed on a railway journey; you pay one, two, or three pence for an insurance ticket; and if you lose your life by an accident during that journey, your representatives will receive two, five, or ten hundred pounds. You may insure for a single journey, a double journey, or for all journeys within a stated definite time. Again, railway servants, and others who travel much, can in like manner be insured, but at higher rates of premium, on account of the higher risk. Nor is this all; if the insurer suffers personal injury without loss of life, he receives compensation for medical services and loss of time. This system is really what it professes to be."[8]

A serious accident occurred on the Eastern Counties Railway in January 1854 near to the town of Thetford, when heavy snow blocked the line. Several gangs of labourers were detailed to move from place to place, clearing the snow to open the line for passengers and other traffic, and "the ordinary regulations of the up and down lines appear to have been disregarded – the main object being to secure a thoroughfare, some part of the way on one line and some part on the other." A train from Cambridge, consisting of two engines and three carriages, arrived at Thetford Station at 4pm in the afternoon. A mail train was also at the station, having been held to await the arrival of the Cambridge train. The two trains then proceeded on their journey, both travelling on the up line, the mail following the Cambridge train at an interval of several minutes. On nearing the place of the disaster the driver of the leading engine noted that another train was approaching, but he assumed that an order had been given that no train should leave Harling station on the up line, so he continued without attempting to stop. A hideous collision occurred, both trains being headed by two engines. These engines were thrown into the air and the two carriages were crushed. Subsequently the corpses of two Firemen, a platelayer, and a carpenter were removed from the wreckage and taken to Harling station, whilst the seriously injured were taken to Thetford station by the mail train.[9]

A further accident on the Eastern Counties Railway, caused by negligence, occurred in 1860, whilst a train was running through Tottenham station. The wheel tyre on the engine broke and the train became derailed, and as a consequence seven passengers lost their lives. The accident was caused by a defective weld, which should have been detected when maintenance work was being undertaken. Partly as a result of this accident, railway wheel tyres ceased to be welded, and continuous rings of cast steel were introduced that could be shrunk on to the wheels.[10]

In August 1862 the Great Eastern Railway Company took over the responsibility for East Anglian railways. Railway safety should have been a priority for the new company, but in 1866 the first fatality occurred.

> "There was a frightful accident on the Great Eastern Railway on Saturday, near to Ely. The train was one which carries passengers at cheap rates from Peterborough to Yarmouth and Lowestoft. Near Ely, while rounding a curve, the engine left the rails and ran down an embankment. The carriages were heaped upon each other in fearful disorder. The driver of the engine was killed, and several of the passengers were much injured."[11]

This accident was followed by another serious derailment at Kelvedon in 1872. The 11.35 up train from Ipswich, which consisted of seven carriages and two guards' breaks, was approaching Kelvedon station at 40 miles per hour when a carriage derailed, causing the engine and tender to leave the rails, and wrecked carriages to be strewn along the side of an embankment. The permanent way was torn up for a distance of approximately 150 yards, with some of the twisted rails becoming entangled with the wheels of the engine. One woman was killed and many people were injured in this accident.[12]

Two years later, in 1874, the worst accident to occur in 19th century East Anglia happened near Thorpe. A collision occurred on the evening of 10th September on the East Norfolk branch of the Great Eastern Railway between a mail train from Yarmouth, and the down express from London.[13] The six miles of railway between Norwich and Brundall consisted of a single line which was controlled by electric telegraph. Because the down express from London was late in arriving at Thorpe station, the night Inspector, Cooper, instructed the Telegraph Clerk to send a message to Brundall, the next station east of Norwich, for the mail to be sent on. Inexplicably, when the down express from London eventually arrived at Thorpe, the engine driver was then allowed to proceed towards Brundall. The mistake was soon realised, but when Robson, the Telegraph Clerk, sent an urgent message to Brundall saying "Hold the mail", the deadly reply came back, "Mail left". A hideous collision occurred when the trains met between the Yare Bridge and the East Norfolk Junction. Both engine crews were killed, "but on the engine of the up Mail, the 7ft single No. 54, they found the regulator shut and the tender brake screwed down hard." In all, a total of 25 people were killed and 73 were injured in the Thorpe disaster.[14]

The fitting of Westinghouse brakes to Great Eastern Railway trains towards the end of the 19th century helped to prevent serious accidents from occurring. The effectiveness of this braking system was demonstrated in September 1907, when the 7.12pm train from Liverpool Street broke in two as it neared Widford in Essex. The division of the train caused the vacuum brake to act, and both portions were brought to a standstill. The train of 19 coaches was afterwards re-coupled and continued on its journey.[14A]

The design of steam engines made rapid progress during the latter part of the 19th century. However, little was known about the design of engine boilers, which were required to operate under pressure. In the 1850s there were virtually no textbooks on boilers that were of any real use, and in drawing offices and workshops there was still much to be learned about boiler design.[15] The earliest boiler rings were of iron plates that were curved by beating or rolling and then riveted together. Lap joints were used, but these proved to be unsuitable for high working pressures.[16] This lack of design knowledge caused many lives to be lost, as in the early days of steam railways boiler explosions were frequent.

The Eastern Counties Railway suffered its first boiler explosion in 1852, when on 25th September a defective plate on one of its locomotives caused the firebox roof to be blown off. No deaths were recorded, but the fireman sustained a hand injury.[17] A further series of explosions, none of which caused fatalities, occurred in 1861. The incidents were reported to the Editor of the *Ipswich Journal* by an irate passenger:

> "There is a short branch line in connection with the main line at Bentley, named the Hadleigh Branch. Happy they who know nothing of the ills attending those to whom it is compulsory to adopt that line of rail. On Monday morning last, May 6th, the would-be passengers on their way to town were alarmed, on alighting at the station, by an escape of steam from the engine, and then discouraged by the announcement from the officials that the locomotive had burst.
>
> Now, Mr Editor, were this a solitary case, your correspondent would not at this moment be appealing to you to publish his wrongs. But, can you believe it, that the Hadleigh engine has blown up four times within the last month or six weeks. Why it is the common talk, that when engines are getting rickety and unsuited for work on the main line, they are transferred to the branches."[18]

The worst East Anglian boiler explosion occurred on the Great Eastern Railway at Westerfield on 25th September 1900. The engine involved was number 522, which was heading the 7.15am goods train from Ipswich to Felixstowe, and consisted of the engine and tender, 34 wagons, and two brake vans. This train drew up at the down home signal at Westerfield station on the far side of the level crossing gates, and whilst waiting for the signal to proceed a violent explosion occurred. The boiler of the engine was thrown over the level crossing, landing on the down platform, and knocking down a signal post and a telegraph pole in the process. A gate-keeper's hut was also demolished, injuring a policeman and a newspaper boy who were standing nearby.[19] "The driver and the fireman of the engine were both killed, the former being blown backwards a distance of 46 yards from the engine, and the body of the latter being found about 20 minutes after the explosion in the third wagon from the engine."[20] Neither the tender nor any other part of the train was damaged by the explosion.

The boiler of engine number 522 was the first boiler with a steel barrel to be involved in an explosion. It was relatively new, and was based at Ipswich after being delivered from Stratford works on 19th September 1899.[21] The subsequent investigation found that poor maintenance was responsible for the accident. When leakages occurred in the firebox of the engine, the repairs were often carried out in an unsatisfactory manner, and the driver's report book showed that leakages had occurred frequently.

| During June 1900 | – | 7 leakages |
| During July 1900 | – | 15 leakages |
| During August 1900 | – | 21 leakages |
| During September 1900 | – | 17 leakages (up to 25th)[22] |

The increasing number of railway accidents throughout the 19th century prompted the press to point out that railway workers were most at risk of death when accidents occurred. In 1896 the following article on railway safety appeared in *The Graphic*:

"To learn on the authority of the Board of Trade, that the number of persons killed and wounded on the railways in the United Kingdom last year were 91 and 99 less than the year before is satisfactory as far as it goes. But it does not go very far, seeing that the total number of the killed was 1,024 and that of the injured 4,021. Nervous persons may, at first sight, be inclined to imagine that railway travelling is a much more dangerous practice than they had previously supposed. Analysis of the figures, however, will suffice to dissipate that misconception of the situation. It is not the passengers who get killed or injured, at least, in the large majority of cases; it is the railway employee. The number of passengers killed by accidents to trains, rolling stock, permanent way, and so forth was only five, while only 399 were injured from those causes. Allowing for the passengers killed or injured in other ways, the proportion of employees to passengers is more than four to one. From this fact a very obvious conclusion may be drawn. It is clear that even now, after three-quarters of a century of experience of railways, and the working of the traffic upon them, we have not done very much to ensure the safety of railway servants. When all reasonable allowance has been made for the perpetual growth of traffic, and the extension of our railways, and consequent increase of risk, the broad fact remains – and it is not to the national credit."[23]

# 9

## Carriages and Locomotives

At the time of the opening of the Eastern Counties Railway between London and Colchester, the engine stock consisted of 35 four-wheeled engines with inside bearings, each weighing in working order about ten or 11 tons and costing, including tender, about £1,600.[1] However, the railway company soon acquired other engines from the firm of Robert Stephenson and Company. The first long boiler engines tended to sway from side to side and were unsteady unless driven at the lowest speeds. Stephenson made improvements by re-building the engine as a 2-4-0 locomotive, but the long boiler type proved to be most successful as a goods locomotive because high speeds were not required.[2]

The line from London to Colchester was eventually extended to Norwich by the Eastern Union Railway. This company operated mainly 2-2-2 and 0-4-2 locomotives that had been purchased from Sharp Bros. & Co, Stothert & Slaughter, and R & W Hawthorn. One engine was, however, unique in that it had been on display at the Great Exhibition of 1851 before being purchased by the Eastern Union Railway.[3] This engine, named 'Ariel's Girdle', was built by the firm of Kitson Thompson and Hewitson and was a 2-2-0 well tank locomotive with outside cylinders and a 304 gallon tank. A long pipe in front of the smokebox acted as the water inlet for the tank, which was located beneath the boiler. As with all of the other Eastern Union Railway engines, 'Ariel's Girdle' used coke as fuel.[4]

Between 1848 and 1859 the Eastern Counties Railway took over the working of the East Anglian, Eastern Union, East Suffolk, Newmarket, and Norfolk Railways.[5] The locomotives of the East Anglian Railway, which were passed to the Eastern Counties Railway, consisted of eight passenger engines and two goods engines, and these were listed in the 1905 edition of the *Locomotive Magazine*:

| East Anglian Railway | Eastern Counties Railway | Names | Dates built |
|---|---|---|---|
| 1 | 108 | Eagle | 1846 |
| 2 | 109 | Vulture | 1846 |
| 3 | 110 | Ostrich | 1846 |
| 4 | 111 | Falcon | 1846 |
| 5 | 112 | Hawk | 1847 |
| 6 | 113 | Kite | 1847 |
| 7 | 114 | Raven | 1847 |
| 8 | 115 | Heron | 1847 |
| 13 Goods | 162 | Lion | 1848 |
| 14 Goods | 164 | Tiger | 1848 |

The passenger engines were all of the 'Sharp single' design with all the wheels having outside bearings. The goods engines were also manufactured by the firm of Sharp Bros, but were of front-coupled design and all of the wheels had inside bearings.[6]

In 1847 the Eastern Counties Railway acquired an unusual locomotive, which was given the name of 'Little Wonder' – the Lilliputian Locomotive Engine. It was constructed for the purpose of inspecting various portions of the railway system, and consisted of an engine and carriage set on four wheels with an overall length of 12ft 6ins. On a trial trip it reached a speed of 43 miles per hour.[7]

Sparks and cinders dropped from the early locomotives often caused fires that damaged line-side property. The problem could be limited by fitting a spark arrester; however, most engines did not have this equipment. In the event of a fire, the railway companies were obliged to reimburse landowners, and sometimes the damage caused was considerable. In 1863 a bridge at Ely was destroyed by a fire caused by either a dropped cinder or a spark from a passing engine. The traffic had to be temporarily suspended, but "arrangements have been made by which the inconvenience will be very much lessened."[8] In 1877 a Farmer took the Great Eastern Railway Company to court when a spark from a locomotive caused a fire which destroyed a crop of barley. The company argued that it had taken all reasonable precautions to prevent sparks starting fires, and that it was not therefore liable. However, the Farmer was awarded the sum of £200.[9]

On 7th August 1862 an Act was passed under which the Eastern Counties Railway and all of its constituent railways were amalgamated to form the Great Eastern Railway. The Locomotive Superintendent of the Eastern Counties Railway at that time, Robert Sinclair, therefore became Locomotive Superintendent of the Great Eastern Railway, a post that he held until 1865. Sinclair was responsible for the design and construction of the following three classes of locomotives:

> "The class 'Y' 2-4-0 locomotives introduced in 1859, the class 'W' 2-2-2 express locomotives (the famous Sinclair Singles), introduced in 1862, and a 2-4-2 tank class for suburban work, which appeared in 1864. The two first-named classes worked the bulk of the Great Eastern passenger traffic for many years."[10]

Sinclair's Great Eastern Engines were painted pea green with black boiler bands and red lining.

Towards the end of the 19th century there was a considerable increase in railway motive power when in 1882 the design of locomotives was taken over by Thomas W. Worsdell. He insisted that all future locomotives should be built at the Stratford Works, and was responsible for introducing a Royal Blue livery for locomotives. "With this colour scheme came the vermillion buffer beams and coupling rods, gold lettering and cast brass number plates with figures set in relief against a red background."[11] Worsdell spent over three years with the Great Eastern Railway until 1885, when the post of Locomotive Superintendent passed to James Holden. Holden designed several successful locomotives for the Great Eastern before 1900:

> "The largest class of express locomotives... were the 'T19' 7ft 2-4-0's, which handled the bulk of the main-line passenger traffic; but he also produced the 'D27' 2-2-2 locomotives between 1889 and 1893, and the handsome 'P43' 4-2-2's, used almost solely on the Cromer expresses. For goods traffic, there were the famous 0-6-0's, of which some still survive as class 'J15' while he produced classes of 0-6-0 and 2-4-2 tank locomotives for suburban and local duties, and the 'T26' 2-4-0 locomotives for mixed traffic."[12]

The earliest carriages on the East Anglian railways were mostly six-wheeled vehicles to accommodate first, second and third class passengers. First and second class accommodation was the equivalent of travelling inside or outside on stage or mail coaches, but third class passengers equated to those who could only afford to travel by stage wagon, or who otherwise resorted to walking. Third class railway wagons in the early days acted as a deterrent to travellers, for they were without seats and roofs.[13] The appalling travelling conditions for passengers using third class accommodation led to an Act being passed by W. E. Gladstone in 1844, which obliged all railway companies "to run one train at least over each trunk, branch, or junction line, at least once each way daily at a minimum of 12mph, stopping if required at all stations, and carrying passengers for one penny a mile or less in carriages with seats and protected from the weather."[14] These trains became known as Parliamentary trains. However, despite Gladstone's Act, open or open-sided vehicles continued to be built for use on excursion trains, and in the 1850s several were constructed for use on the Eastern Counties Railway. Fourth-class accommodation, which basically consisted of wooden trucks, was also used on the Eastern Counties and Norfolk Railways in 1853. These fourth class carriages ran between Yarmouth and London.[15]

Height restrictions made access to the early carriages difficult for tall passengers, who often bumped their heads, "but it should be remembered that the height of British passenger vehicles was for long restricted by the very general practice of placing the luggage in a tarpaulin-covered pile on the roof."[16] The October 1913 edition of the *Great Eastern Railway Magazine* carried a reproduction from the *Illustrated London News,* which showed the arrival of an Eastern Counties Christmas train at Shoreditch in 1849. Porters can be seen offloading luggage from the carriage roofs, and also from a luggage van attached to the train.

The fares charged by the Eastern Counties Railway for first, second and third class carriages were 3d, 2d, and 1d per mile, and average receipts were about £28 per mile per week. For third class carriages with seats, a slightly higher fare than 1d per mile was charged, but the majority of the passengers who travelled third class were quite content to travel standing.[17] Smoking was strictly prohibited by most of the railway companies, but in 1846 the Eastern Counties Railway introduced special smoking saloons, which were quite luxuriously appointed, much to the annoyance of non-smokers who felt that their accommodation was inferior. These smoking carriages were six-wheelers, mounted on composite wooden wheels with Bridges Adams bowsprings. "The saloon itself was approached from two open, unroofed compartments, one at each end... and the large windows of half-inch plate glass with red silk roller blinds afforded uninterrupted views of the gracious villages and magnificent churches which provided the Eastern Counties Railway with its scenic attractions."[18] The *Graphic* newspaper complained about the fact that these saloons were frequented by ladies.

> "Theodore Hook said that to attract a gathering of the fair sex nothing was more efficacious than the announcement of a meeting for the discussion of some topic of peculiarly masculine interest, and to request the attendance of gentlemen only. We are reminded of this reflection by the fact that the railway smoking carriages are continually frequented by ladies. The dear creatures seem to have an especial fondness for intruding where their presence is inappropriate. If you venture to remind them of their supposed mistake, they graciously assure you that they have no objection to your smoking; but they do not take into consideration how many smokers are deprived of their accustomed solace, simply because they are driven to ordinary carriages from the mere want of room in those especially prepared for them. If passengers who enter a non-smoking carriage, and do smoke, are to be fined 40 shillings and costs, surely by inverse logic those that use a smoking carriage, and do not smoke, should be liable to a similar infliction."[19]

In the early days the Eastern Union Railway ran through Ipswich to Colchester, where passengers for Shoreditch were transferred to the Eastern Counties Railway. The Eastern Union Railway had, however, second class carriages which were far superior to those run by the Eastern Counties, and consequently the Eastern Counties banned these vehicles from running through to Shoreditch in case their own first class traffic should suffer. Second class passengers were therefore forced to vacate their comfortable carriages at Colchester and transfer to Eastern Counties 'tumbrels'.[20]

The Eastern Union Railway purchased their second class carriages from an Ipswich firm, Messrs Catt & Quadling. The carriages had their seats and backs covered with leather cushions, and the doors and side openings were furnished with glass windows. These luxuries for second class passengers were almost unheard of at that time.[21]

In 1847, Her Majesty Queen Victoria and the Prince Consort travelled on the Eastern Counties Railway for the first time when they travelled from Tottenham to Cambridge in connection with the Installation of the Prince as Chancellor of Cambridge University. The Eastern Counties Company had no royal saloon or even a carriage that was considered suitable, so they obtained one for the occasion from the London and North Western Railway. The special train, besides the royal saloon, consisted of three first class carriages and two brake vans, and was preceded by a pilot engine that bore the Union Jack, whilst the engine of the royal train carried two similar emblems.[22]

When the Great Eastern Railway eventually took over the running of East Anglian services, the second class carriages operated by this company were the subject of a contentious complaint to the press:

"GREAT EASTERN RAILWAY CARRIAGES

Sir, - It is difficult to see how the Directors of the Great Eastern Railway can justify their retention of the hard-seated, cushionless-backed, and crutchless second class carriages which they still employ on their lines.

That the same rate should be charged for this miserable accommodation that passengers on the London & North Western, Great Western and Midland lines pay for the roomy and comfortable carriages provided by those companies, seems a base imposition upon the public.

There are many whose means do not admit of their habitually travelling first class, and yet to whom a certain degree of comfort in a long journey is almost essential. This, by the payment of a sum nearly twice a third class fare, they might reasonably expect to secure.

Yours faithfully,
M. A."

But this view was not shared by everybody and the above-mentioned letter drew the following response:

> "Sir, - Your correspondent 'M. A.' whose letter you published yesterday, seems to have a very distorted idea of the accommodation afforded to second-class passengers by the Great Eastern Railway.
>
> I have been a frequent traveller on that line for the last 20 years, via Ipswich to Yarmouth, and I unhesitatingly assert that for many years past there have been second-class carriages to the greater part of the trains equal to those of any other great line.
>
> 'M. A.' must I fancy, have mistaken the class, and travelled in a third class carriage, which would account for the discomfort he seems to have suffered.
>
> Yours faithfully,<br>J. M. D."[23]

The Great Eastern Railway introduced a six-wheeled passenger coach towards the end of the 19th century. The coach consisted of both first and second class compartments with a separate compartment for luggage. However, on 1st January 1893, second class disappeared from most Great Eastern trains. It remained only on London suburban services and continental expresses.[24]

# 10

## Passengers

Whilst the average speed of the early railway trains was only 28 to 30 miles per hour, this was considerably faster than the speeds attained on the roads by stagecoaches. The increased speed of travel shortened journey times, thereby increasing the mobility of people living in rural areas. Consequently, despite the fact that railway travel was expensive, passenger numbers increased rapidly. The total number of passengers carried on Britain's railways increased from 24.5 million in 1842 to nearly 73 million in 1850 and 507 million in 1875."

The Eastern Counties Railway drew the majority of its passengers from towns and villages in rural areas, but these passengers tended to travel relatively short distances. These rural areas certainly provided a regular flow of passengers; however, the numbers travelling were not sufficient to generate large profits as the high fares forced many people to travel on the 'Parliamentary' trains, which carried third class passengers and stopped at all stations. In its early years, the Eastern Counties Railway was forced to terminate at Colchester instead of Ipswich because of financial difficulties. Eventually the financial difficulties were overcome and the railway was extended throughout East Anglia, but by this time the company had acquired a poor reputation. Some people may have been reluctant to travel after reading the derisory articles about the railway company published in magazines such as *Punch*:

> "On Wednesday last, a respectably dressed young man was seen to go to the Shoreditch terminus Eastern Counties Railway and deliberately take a ticket for Cambridge. He has not since been heard of. No motive has been assigned for his rash act."[2]

The railway companies were not initially anxious to attract third class passengers. Class snobbery fostered the belief that "the behaviour of third-class passengers caused offence to other classes of passengers... the belief that the 'lower orders' would annoy, even drive away higher class patrons, or simply vandalise railway property was a recurring theme in railway history."[3] This attitude was certainly shared by the travelling public, some of whom felt sufficiently strongly about the matter to send letters to local newspapers concerning the intrusion of third-class passengers into second class accommodation:

> "THE COMFORT OF RAILWAY PASSENGERS
> To the Editor of the *Norfolk News*
> Sir – Many of your readers have doubtless like myself been annoyed when travelling as second class passengers on the Great Eastern Railway, by the intrusion of the company's workmen, in a state neither clean nor sweet, into the compartment in which they are seated. Some of them may not have courage to appeal to the Guard, or, when told by him that if they don't like their company they may seek another compartment, to apply to the Station Master, as I did the other day and obtain their instant removal. I have moreover written to the Chairman, and in his absence I have now before me a note from the Superintendent, who informs me that "there is a positive rule on this line, that the company's workmen shall travel in third-class carriages, and in the event of the train being only first and second class, that they shall be placed in second-class compartments by themselves, apart from the other passengers." This rule is plain enough, and if you will only give it publicity by insertion in your columns, you will assist the company in enforcing its observance and contribute to the ease and comfort of the public. It is due to the other guards in the company's employ to state that the train by which I travelled left Ipswich for London at 1.25pm on Saturday, the 14th instant.
> 
>        I am, your obedient servant,
>     Oct 18, 1865                   VIATOR"[4]

Despite the hostility shown towards third class passengers, third class travel had become important to the railway companies by the latter part of the 19th century. Gladstone's Railway Act of 1844 had initiated the growth of third class travel with the introduction of Parliamentary trains, and the popularity of excursions had attracted large numbers of passengers, many of whom could only afford third class accommodation. The degeneration of the inner districts of large cities, which had come about because of the need to demolish housing to enable railway construction to take place, resulted in the railway companies having to offer workmen's tickets so that working families could live on the outskirts of a city, whilst the men could travel into work at a cheap rate. Although in 1883 the Cheap Trains Act was passed, which enabled the Board of Trade to compel the railway companies to offer concessionary fares, it proved to be unnecessary as most companies ran more trains for workmen than they were required to do under the terms of the Act. The Great Eastern Railway was praised for its cheap and frequent services, allowing workers to travel in from as far out as Walthamstow, seven miles from Liverpool Street, at fares of between 2d and 4d.[5] These workmen's services mixed people of different social classes, and even the General Manager of the Great Eastern Railway was forced to admit that "I should be very sorry indeed to allow any respectable female connected with my household to travel third-class upon the Great Eastern Railway during those hours of the day in which the workers are travelling."[6]

Obnoxious passengers were not only found in third class carriages. As the numbers of travellers increased it was often necessary to travel in crowded railway compartments where an inconsiderate passenger could cause chaos:

> "An individual – I cannot bring myself to allude to him as a man – has just entered the compartment who has made me think for the hundredth time that it would be a good thing if a law were passed precluding certain types from travelling in railway trains. He has trodden on the feet of every occupant of the carriage; he has countless pieces of luggage, a hacking cough, and a dog of distinctly warlike appearance. He has favoured every one of us with a sombre scowl which is intended to indicate that he regards us one

and all as interlopers, and now that he has settled himself to slumber he proves to be the possessor of a snore of thunderous dimensions. I must, when I get back to town, look up the law on justifiable homicide."[7]

It has been estimated that towards the end of the 19th century over 500 million railway journeys were being made each year throughout the United Kingdom. It is therefore not surprising that the railway companies were the recipients of a vast assortment of lost property that had been left in railway carriages by the travelling public. As most of this lost property remained unclaimed, it was usual for the railway companies to periodically hold sales at which the goods were sold to the public at very low prices.

> "Twelve coats, 13 shillings; six pairs of trousers and three vests, eight shillings; 12 waterproof ladies' cloaks, ten shillings; 30 pieces skirts and dress bodies, seven shillings; 12 white shirts, seven shillings; two pairs of white drill trousers, two ditto coats, and 15 pairs of drawers, three shillings; 22 chemises, nine shillings; 18 ladies' under-jackets and six night-dresses, eight shillings; a dressing gown, pair of ladies' capes, and seven pairs of stays. Dirt cheap at five shillings, ladies – gone!"[8]

*The Graphic* newspaper, in commenting on lost property found in railway carriages, drew attention to the amount of luggage carried by women when travelling by train:

> "We need not be hard upon the gentler sex, and attribute to it more forgetfulness than is exhibited by the masculine. The truth is that women provide a greater number of separate packages than men when setting out on a journey, and are thereby liable to a greater number and variety of slips of memory. Women have much to do with the five B's (the alliteration is accidental), boxes, bags, baskets, bundles, and babies, and may forget one or all of them in turns (except babies; did a woman ever leave her infant behind

through sheer forgetfulness?). Ladies' purses are often left in a compartment of a carriage, after a desperate attempt to find the railway ticket. As to wearing apparel, men and women have alike to blame themselves for much remissness when travelling. Hats laid aside temporarily for soft caps, overcoats placed on the seat, railway rugs forgotten when removed from their wanted position as wrappers, mantles, shawls, scarfs, tippets, muffs, bows, comforters, cloaks, gloves, handkerchiefs, all are in peril of passing into oblivion during the hurried exit of passengers from railway carriages. Boxes, trunks, portmanteaux – who can tell how many of these come to grief through forgetfulness, or how many small miseries may attend the loss of wearing apparel as a consequence?"[9]

In view of the large amount of luggage carried by Victorian travellers the railway company introduced the 'Luggage in Advance' scheme. This enabled a passenger to complete a green luggage form, obtained at a booking office, giving details of date, destination, number of packages and description of contents. Once completed and handed over, an appropriate number of labels were issued and a charge of 2/- per item of luggage was then levied. The luggage was subsequently collected by a horse-drawn van operated by the railway company, and taken to the station. The passenger was therefore spared the inconvenience of carrying his or her luggage on the journey, and the railway company was able to transport the luggage at the most convenient time.[10]

It was hoped that the introduction of workmen's tickets would lead to an exodus of working class families from the city centre into the surrounding suburbs; however, this did not immediately take place. There were a number of reasons as to why the use of workmen's tickets increased at a slow rate. Firstly, the rents in many suburban areas were too high for working class families to afford, and in some areas a supply of suitable property was not readily available. Secondly, leaving a home in the city meant moving away from family and friends, both of whom could provide support in times of need. It was also necessary for some workmen to live near to their place of work, as tools were often shared. In addition, some of the work undertaken was either seasonal or intermittent so that there was no need for a regular workmen's ticket. The railway companies also found that the operation of workmen's trains was not particularly profitable. However, the Great Eastern Railway company was prepared to tolerate losses on its workman's trains because "indirectly they pay us. The workmen's wives and families, and the tradesmen who serve them, travel up and down the line at ordinary fares."[11]

It was mainly the middle classes, who were better paid, who were able to take advantage of cheaper fares, and move to suburban areas, and by the time of the First World War daily commuting to work had become an established practice. The Clacton season ticket holders held an annual dinner to which members of the Great Eastern Railway were invited:

"Clacton Season Ticket Holders

The annual dinner of the above on May 1st at the Grand Hotel was a great success. Mr Jos. May was in the chair, and among the Great Eastern visitors were Mr W. J. Galloway, Mr H. W. Thornton and Mr H. C. Amendt. This was Mr Thornton's first opportunity of meeting a large body of Great Eastern passengers, and he received a hearty welcome, which was none the less sincere because he came with gifts in his hands in the form of improvements in the train service. In replying to the toast of the Great Eastern Railway, Mr Galloway and Mr Thornton both referred to the identity of interests of the company and the towns on its system, and Mr Thornton welcomed the formation of passengers' associations, because he said it enabled the railway to find out definitely the needs of each community. The proceedings terminated with a concert in the hotel lounge."[12]

# 11

# LEVEL CROSSINGS

It was often necessary for the early railway lines to cross roads that were used by horse-drawn vehicles and pedestrians. In East Anglia the railway engineers were fortunate in being able to lay their lines across relatively flat land, so bridge construction at crossing points was unnecessary, and consequently these crossing points became known as 'level crossings'.

The speed of trains on the early railways was not excessive, so there was little danger of accidents occurring on the first level crossings. However, as the railways progressed, the speed of trains increased, and it became obvious that there was a significant risk of a collision, particularly in view of the lengthy stopping distance that trains required. In order to minimise this risk, gates were erected on either side of the line, and these gates were normally closed across the road, only being opened when someone wanted to cross the railway. A gatekeeper was employed to open and close the gates, and at some crossings he also lighted, trimmed and cleaned the lamps on the crossing gates. The job necessitated being on duty for 24 hours, seven days per week, so a cottage was usually provided by the railway company. Sometimes the job was given to a railwayman who had been injured whilst carrying out his duties and could therefore no longer continue in his job. The gatekeeper often shared his duties with his wife. In his book on the East Suffolk Railway, John Brodribb notes that generations of the same family often worked on the railway. He gives as an example the Punchard family, and their work on the East Suffolk Railway:

> "The railway history of the Punchard family started with William, born at Halesworth in 1837. In 1872 he changed jobs from agricultural labourer to platelayer on the Great Eastern, living in the gate house at North Green, Kelsale, with his wife Sarah who was the gatekeeper. She died of hypertrophy of the heart on the 25th May 1895, age 56,

having borne many children. William Punchard's obituary in the *GER magazine* noted that he 'died in September last (1922) having retired on the pension fund in 1906 after 34 years' service.' He was widely known and respected in the Darsham area."[1]

The most dangerous type of level crossings were the unmanned crossings connecting farm land or footpaths. An accident on the Great Eastern Railway in the vicinity of Cambridge illustrates this point. In 1870 the 5pm train from Newmarket to Cambridge was proceeding towards Cambridge station when a man driving a horse and cart laden with hurdles attempted to cross in front of the train at a farm level crossing. The engine caught the cart, and it and the hurdles were smashed to pieces. The horse was so injured that it had to be killed on the spot. The driver of the cart was subsequently blamed for the accident.[2] It was recognised that level crossings, in addition to delaying journeys, were a safety risk to land owners, road users, and pedestrians. In addition, they also required regular maintenance, and they were difficult for the elderly and disabled people to use. However, no other method of separating roads from railway lines was available, other than by utilising bridge construction.

Railway employees were probably more at risk from death or injury on level crossings than other members of the public. An accident occurred at Diss Station in November 1883 when a Porter named Fiddeman narrowly escaped being killed whilst standing against an old signal box near to the level crossing. Fiddeman was watching the approach of the 7.27pm down train from London when he was struck by the cylinder of the 7.30pm up train from Norwich, and was thrown a distance of several feet onto the platform. Landing on his head, he received a severe scalp wound from which blood poured. On admission to hospital it was found that he had also sustained internal injuries. Commenting on the accident, the *Ipswich Journal* stated that:

> "The crossing at Diss is a most dangerous one, especially to strangers, and it must be a constant source of anxiety to the Stationmaster and his staff, and notwithstanding that porters are placed there when trains are due to caution people, there

have been several very narrow escapes – one only just previous to this accident – and it is felt by many who use the railway that a larger and more convenient station is necessary, or that a bridge should be placed over the crossing."[3]

Barking station also had a dangerous level crossing, which was built in East Street with gates to control the road traffic. This crossing had 'kissing gates' to allow pedestrians to cross without going through the main gates, and these kissing gates allowed people to try and cross the railway lines when the main gates were closed, leading to several fatal accidents. One victim in 1878 was Edward Maynard, landlord of the Spotted Dog pub, who was deaf and unaware of the train coming. In 1884 a footbridge was built over the track and the pedestrian gates closed.[4] At Stowmarket station the level crossing was located near to sidings where shunting was regularly undertaken. In October 1874 a number of leading landowners took the Great Eastern Railway Company to court because the trucks of a goods train had been allowed to stand across the level crossing whilst shunting was taking place. In view of the fact that it was illegal for a train to stand on a crossing during shunting, the Magistrates found that the case was wholly justified, although the railway company officials considered that they were being harassed.[5]

A further action was brought against the Great Eastern Railway Company about this matter in Suffolk County Court when a Mr Roberts asked for compensation of £50 for unlawful detention at the Stowmarket level crossing. Mr Roberts, a Solicitor, stated that he was detained for six-and-a-half minutes at the crossing, and that he lost the post and a client in consequence. In an attempt to make up time he strained his horse to such an extent that he was unable to use it for six weeks. The Judge said he was of the opinion that there was no remedy against the company to make them discontinue the practice of blocking up level crossings by action, but there was by criminal indictment. In order to determine the course of action to be pursued he asked the jury to consider three points:

> "…whether the loss of the client as Mr Roberts had sworn to was the natural consequence which might be expected to result from the stoppage; whether Mr Roberts would have arrived in time without the stoppage; and whether the

overdriving of the horse was the natural consequence of the stoppage at the gate at the station. The jury returned a verdict on all points in favour of the plaintiff, awarding £15 for the loss sustained in respect of the horse, and £10 for the loss sustained in respect of the client."[6]

Although there were many complaints from the public about the dangers posed by station level crossings, particularly during shunting operations, in general station crossings were adequately supervised. Some were located near to a signal box which enabled the signalman to provide an additional level of supervision. When in 1885 the Board of Trade investigated an accident which had occurred on the level crossing at Halstead station, local traders and others held a meeting at which the following resolution was passed:

"That this meeting regrets that an unfair and one-sided memorial has been presented to the Board of Trade with respect to the accident which occurred recently at the railway crossing in Trinity Street; that this meeting expresses its strong conviction that the company have taken reasonable precautions to minimise the inconvenience and danger which arise from the necessary shunting and passing of carriages at the crossing, and that great care has been exercised in this respect is evident from the fact that notwithstanding the proximity of the crossing to the station, not a single accident has until now occurred during the period of 27 years. That this meeting presents its thanks to the directors and manager of the Colne Valley Railway for the facilities which they have afforded the town of Halstead with regard to both passenger and merchandise traffic; and that a memorial from inhabitants interested in this question be presented to the directors of the Colne Valley Railway and to the Board of Trade, embodying these views."[7]

Gatekeeper pay grades were amongst the lowest for railway workers. However, a gatekeeper was entitled to a rent-free cottage in addition to wages whilst undertaking his duties. Living near to the level crossing was essential as it enabled the gatekeeper to operate the crossing gates and sometimes to operate signals or points. The rates paid to gatekeepers are given in 'Victorian Railwaymen' as follows:

|  | Average s – d | Range s – d |  | s – d |
|---|---|---|---|---|
| Early 1840s | 13  5 | 12  0 | - | 21  0 |
| Late  1840s | 13  2 | 12  0 | - | 17  6 |
| 1850s | 12  3 | 9  0 | - | 17  0 |
| 1860s | 12  10 | 10  0 | - | 20  0 |
| Early 1870s | 11  2 | 10  0 | - | 0  0 |

It can be seen that gatekeeper rates of pay decreased slightly during the course of the 19th century.[8]

Railway work was dangerous and accidents were frequent; however, the railway companies in East Anglia provided secure employment. Consequently, many agricultural workers, who faced insecurity in their employment, abandoned agriculture for better paid jobs on the railways. However, these relatively unskilled men found themselves in responsible positions where they were expected to work long hours. The long hours of work often resulted in men sleeping on the job or being drunk whilst on duty, but discipline was strict and these offences usually led to instant dismissal. However, if a railway worker was injured and unable to carry on his normal duties he was often transferred to the post of gatekeeper. As an example of this "one labourer on the Great Northern in 1850 who lost his arm on duty was paid 10s per week for nine weeks, had a donation of three guineas, payment of surgeon's fees of seven guineas, and was re-employed as a gateman at a lower rate of wages."[9]

Gatekeepers had often held a variety of railway jobs before they were finally made responsible for a level crossing. Unlike most 19th century occupations, railwaymen were expected to work in different locations during the course of their service if they wished to gain promotion. In June 1914 the *Great Eastern Railway Magazine* reported the following retirement:

"Mr George Masters, Gateman, Heacham, retired in March last at the age of 74. He joined the Eastern Counties Railway in January, 1858, as lad porter at Wimblington, and during his 56 years' service he has held varying positions at no less than ten stations, occupying the positions of lad-porter, signalman, foreman porter, and gateman respectively. He was appointed Gateman at Heacham in January, 1906, and now looks forward to a period of quiet retirement there."[10]

It was usual for railwaymen who were retiring to receive a presentation of some sort from their colleagues, and usually this took the form of a cash gift, or a useful article such as a travelling bag or an umbrella. The following presentation was therefore somewhat unusual:

"Mr W. Smith, Platelayer, retired on 14th February after 49 years' service, 40 of which were spent at Brundall. He has been presented with half a ton of coal, five stone of flour, pipe, tobacco and cash balance, subscribed by friends at Brundall and surrounding stations. Mr Miles the Station Master, made the presentation."[11]

# 12

# INDUSTRIAL RELATIONS

The early railway companies faced a dilemma with regard to the employment of labour. Railways needed to be as safe as possible for both the travelling public and for the railway operatives. Drunkenness, carelessness, sleeping on the job and unauthorised absences could therefore not be tolerated; however, skilled labour was not initially available as most new applicants were labourers with an agricultural background. In order to make their railways as safe as possible the companies introduced rigid disciplinary regimes in order to ensure that railway work was carried out safely in accordance with established procedures and company regulations.

In the 1840s the penalties for breach of company regulations were severe. Dismissals were frequent, particularly for being drunk or asleep whilst on duty. Sometimes fines were levied for lesser offences, but it was often the case that the offender was taken before a Justice of the Peace and subsequently jailed. The law allowed railway companies to act in accordance with the disciplinary procedures set out in the 1840 Railway Act, as amended in 1842.[1] The disciplinary clauses in this Act, and in subsequent Acts, were incorporated in the rule book of the Eastern Counties Railway Company as follows:

> "The non-observance of any of the foregoing Regulations will subject the Offender to Fines and to prosecution under Lord Seymour's Act for the Better Regulation of Railways.
>
> No instance of intoxication will be overlooked and any man dismissed from the Company's service for that offence will be liable to a fine by the magistrate.
>
> Ordered that in every case of infringement of Rules or departures from them the persons offending be immediately suspended and reported to the Directors so that in case of grave offence the parties may be discharged or prosecuted.

> Before any person is employed he shall be required to sign these regulations and for disobedience of which he will be punished as for an offence against his Employers and against the Law.
>
> Enginemen are informed that instructions have been given to immediately arrest and convey before a magistrate, any engine driver or other person who shall disobey the Stopping or Caution signals.
>
> No instance of intoxication on duty will ever be overlooked, and besides being dismissed the offender will be liable to be punished by the magistrate."[2]

Because there were no trade unions for railwaymen in the 1840s, it was difficult to register a grievance with the railway company. It was usual to submit a petition to the Directors; however, these usually met with limited success. Strike action was rare because it usually resulted in dismissal; however, the first strike on the Eastern Counties Railway occurred in December 1839 when the engine drivers and stokers, together with the platelayers, refused to work because of a dispute over wages. The engineer in charge of the line consulted with the directors and an agreement was reached to enable the traffic to be resumed without any further trouble.[3] In August 1850 a much more serious dispute arose when Mr Gooch, the new Locomotive Superintendent, issued new regulations and levied disciplinary fines on the engine drivers and firemen for non-compliance. This led to a deputation visiting Mr Ellis, one of the Directors, to state the hardships of the new regulations, and in consequence of the unsatisfactory nature of the interview 178 of the men sent in their resignations.[4] As a result of this, all of the drivers and firemen were dismissed and advertisements were placed in the press for replacements. On 20th August 1850 Mr Gooch sent a letter to *The Times* concerning the resignations:

> "The reason they assigned for so doing, in the memorial they presented you on the same day, was the unjust fines which had been imposed upon them by me. You are fully aware that, in conducting an establishment of this character and magnitude, the strictest discipline is necessary to insure

safety to the travelling public, as well as economy to the shareholders. It is with great regret I am compelled to say that, on taking charge of this department of your railway a few weeks ago, I found the discipline throughout the whole extent in a very unsatisfactory state."[5]

Drivers were recruited from other railway companies to take over the operation of Eastern Counties engines. These strike-breaking drivers were assisted by guards, the upper guards being awarded three guineas whilst under guards and porters received £1 15s 0d each.[6] The Eastern Counties Company subsequently issued a poster containing a black list of 90 drivers and 87 firemen who had struck.[7] The employment of inexperienced drivers on the Eastern Counties railways led to some frightening incidents which could have resulted in death or serious injury. In August 1850 the down Parliamentary train from London arrived at Norwich Station, two hours late at 2.45pm. The new driver unhooked his engine in front of the train, "and was shunting back onto the next line in order to proceed to the end and propel it into the arcade of the terminus. In doing that, however, he came in collision with a pilot engine, and eventually he ended the matter by forcing the train into the terminus with such force as to throw the passengers about in the carriages with much violence."[8]

Most of the new drivers failed to keep to the timetable, some trains being hours late on arrival. One inexperienced driver ran his engine up and down the down line, passing danger signals at a time when an express train from Norwich was due. A further instance of carelessness arose when the driver of the 12.15pm down train from London ran past Stratford Bridge station without stopping to take up or set down passengers. The passengers who were waiting for this train had their money returned as a result of its not stopping. When the pumps failed on an engine bound for London, the driver put out his fire and attempted to reach Stratford with the remaining steam left in the boiler; however, when the water ran out the engine was left standing at Chelmsford with the tubes and fire box seriously damaged. A replacement engine had to be sent from Stratford to continue the service.[9]

Railway work offered permanent employment, and applicants for the higher graded posts were therefore required to provide referees, and to deposit a sum of money as a security if their employment would involve dealing with money. Although railway work was dangerous, the companies were under no obligation to provide compensation for any injury sustained. However, various forms of *ex-gratia* compensation existed:

> "Payment of wages, during disability and of medical expenses, donations to dependants, funeral allowances, were available; often companies contributed to hospitals, infirmaries, etcetera, and provident societies and accident funds existed which were subsidised by the companies."[10]

During the construction of the Eastern Union Railway a surgeon was under contract to provide medical assistance to the men at a rate of three half pence per week per man, whether sick or well. The average rate of payment to the surgeon was 12s 6d per week. The Eastern Union Railway Company also donated the sum of £50 each to the hospitals in Colchester and Ipswich because of the number of accidents that had occurred, and similar donations were made by the Ipswich and Bury Railway Company to hospitals at each end of its line.[11]

Railway companies also considered the education of their employees to be important, and consequently in 1850 an Eastern Counties school was set up in Stratford for enginemen and artisans.[12] Religious education was also encouraged, and facilities were therefore made available for railwaymen to receive religious instruction. In 1871 the first trade union for railwaymen was formed with the title 'The Amalgamated Society of Railway Servants of England, Ireland, Scotland and Wales'. Initially the union claimed 17,247 members, but internal disputes reduced this figure to 6,300 by 1882. Although the union claimed to represent all types of railway workers it did not recruit general labourers or the craftsmen working in the engineering shops.[13] There is no record of women workers being allowed to join the trade union, although during the course of the 19th century the Great Eastern Railway employed women in its printing and linen departments, and they also served as stewardesses on the continental steamers.[14]

The Great Eastern Railway started a 'Friendly Society' in 1860. This was for railwaymen in the 'Traffic' grades and members made contributions of between 4d and 8d per week. Sickness allowance and accident allowance was set at 8s 0d to 16s 0d per week with a death allowance of £10 to £20. The Great Eastern Railway Company contributed £500 per annum towards the operating expenses; however, in 1863 there were only 392 members of the Friendly Society.[15] In 1898 the Great Eastern Railway Company generated much resentment when it opened a superannuation fund. Membership of the fund was compulsory, but the railwaymen who had to pay had no say in its management and were not allowed to elect any of the men on the committee.

> "Workers at the Great Eastern Railway Company charged that the superannuation fund set up in the 1890s was designed to 'get an undue hold over the men and thus coerce them, and have an influence over them which they (the company) would not possess if the fund was not established.' They also resented the thought that the fund would be used to exert pressure on the servants to remain in the service."[16]

Despite its initial troubles, the superannuation fund proved invaluable to the widows of railwaymen who had died whilst in service. When Frederick Stratton, a goods Guard based at Liverpool Street Station, died on 15th October 1899 he left a widow, Eliza, and one son. Eliza submitted a claim form to the Great Eastern Railway Superannuation Fund on 28th October 1899, together with a Registrar's Certificate of Death and her Marriage Certificate, and on 21st November 1899 she received £78 13s 4d in settlement of her claim.[17]

On 1st January 1908 the Great Eastern Railway Accident Fund was formed. The fund had offices at Liverpool Street Station and it was controlled by a Committee on which "five servants of the Company being members of the fund" were allowed to sit. Membership of the fund was dependent on paying a contribution of 1d per week which was deducted from wages and, unlike the Superannuation Fund, membership of the scheme was not compulsory. In fact, the rule book stated that:

> "Every servant who desires to become a Member shall testify his desire by signing and forwarding to the Secretary an application in the form printed at the foot of these Rules or in such other manner as the Committee may from time to time authorise or require. Upon so testifying his desire the

Servant shall become a Member and his contribution of one penny per week to the Fund to be deducted from his wages according to the Scheme shall immediately commence. Every person becoming a Member shall be entitled to receive free of charge a copy of the Scheme and of these Rules."[18]

Funds of this nature were essential because railway accidents were so frequent, not only throughout the 19th century, but also in the 20th. In 1920 four railway companies jointly published an advisory booklet for railwaymen entitled 'Prevention of Accidents to Staff Engaged in Railway Operation'. The introductory page pointed out that every year between 200 and 300 railwaymen were killed, and in addition several thousand met with accidents. "Investigation of the accidents occurring shows that a high proportion of them are attributable to thoughtlessness or lack of foresight and care, either on the part of the injured person or others".[19] The booklet was illustrated with photographs showing how accidents were likely to occur and showed potential accidents arising from not paying attention when working on railway lines. They also emphasised the dangers involved in the moving or shunting of wagons, the incorrect use of the shunting pole, and incorrect uncoupling practices. The booklet ended with the following warning:

"Just one word to the older members of the staff. Many experienced men have been killed or injured by neglecting to observe simple precautions such as those suggested in this booklet. Frequently it has apparently been a case of 'familiarity breeds contempt'. Do not consider that your experience entitles you to be careless."[20]

# 13

## THE LONDON TERMINI

The Eastern Counties Act, which was dated 4th July 1836, allowed for the construction of 126 miles of railway from London to Yarmouth. However, the progress of construction work on the Eastern Counties Railway was slow, and by 1839 only ten-and-a-half miles of railway between Mile End and Romford had been opened to the public. By this time it was apparent that because of financial difficulties the railway would never reach Yarmouth, and a decision was therefore taken that the railway would terminate at Colchester.[1] Mile End was the nearest location to London for the Eastern Counties Railway, so a station called Devonshire Street was opened on 29th June 1839 to serve as a temporary terminus. However, Devonshire Street did not stay open for long, as the Eastern Counties Railway was soon extended outwards to Brentwood and seven miles inward to a new terminus at Shoreditch. This enabled Devonshire Street Station to close in 1843.[2]

The new Shoreditch terminus was eventually located in a fairly rough area of London. It was not near to either the City or the West End, and throughout its life the station was constantly under redevelopment as it was undersized and unable to cope with the traffic that the main line terminus generated. Eventually, however, Shoreditch became the terminus of the entire Great Eastern system. Line after line was added until it became necessary to erect unsightly sheds on the northern side of the station to cope with the additional traffic caused by the Great Eastern Railway taking over the running of the Tilbury and Southend and the Woolwich lines. "For years it has been customary to send off trains from the arrival platform, and to keep arriving trains waiting, sometimes an inordinate length of time, outside the station. The frequent stoppages, even of express trains, on the road between Stratford and London must, one would think, have familiarised nearly everyone in the Eastern Counties with the by no means magnificent view to be obtained from the carriage windows between these two places."[3]

Despite the lack of capacity, the appearance of the station was considered to be impressive. In *Victorian Stations*, Gordon Biddle describes this Italianate structure as follows:

> "Sancton Wood built the Eastern Counties Railway terminus on arches above street level. At the end of the spacious triple-arched trainshed a heavily corniced three-storey frontage block was built at the head of twin flights of balustraded stairs rising to the entrance on the first floor. In front a broad cab-drive, also balustraded, swept round in a wide semicircle, setting off the entrance to perfection. Alongside the shed a second block was added with a central pediment."[4]

Unfortunately the terminus was a magnet for pickpockets who frequently robbed the passengers.

> "ROBBERIES AT RAILWAY STATIONS
> To the Editor of the *Norfolk Chronicle*
>
> SIR – Permit me through the medium of your columns to caution excursionists against the light-fingered gentry who have of late been infesting the Shoreditch Railway Station, much to the cost of many poor people. Only on Friday last a servant-girl from Norwich, intending to visit the Exhibition, was robbed of all her hard-earned savings (as also her return ticket), thus marring all her contemplated pleasure. It is therefore to be hoped that country people will be upon their guard against these plausible set of villains, who are always on the look-out for plunder.
>
> Your obedient servant,
> WM. F BATLEY
> Pownall Road, Dalston, London. N.E.
> July 30th, 1862
>
> P.S. – In justice to the Railway Company, I must mention that upon my making the case known to them, they generously consented to give the poor girl a free pass back."[5]

## THE COMING OF THE RAILWAYS TO EAST ANGLIA

In 1844 large numbers of staff were appointed to manage the station. The hours of work for the Station Master were from 7.00am until the arrival of the last train, and for the Deputy Station Master the official hours were from 4.45am to 5.30pm. Other grades of staff were recruited, consisting of policemen, takers, watchmen, and point turners, their hours of work being mostly between 7.00am until 9.00pm. Following these appointments in 1846 the Shoreditch terminus was renamed Bishopsgate, presumably in an attempt to make people believe that it was nearer to the centre of the City.[6]

The Eastern Counties Railway found that the carriage of goods into London was a valuable source of revenue, and consequently a small depot was opened near to Bishopsgate and given the name of Brick Lane. Large amounts of agricultural produce from East Anglia arrived at the Brick Lane depot in tarpaulin-covered wagons, and the wheat, barley, oats, beans, and cereals were then taken to two large granaries which the railway company had also constructed near to its terminus.[7] All of these premises became the responsibility of the Great Eastern Railway when in 1862 this company took over the running of East Anglian railways.

In 1866, the Great Eastern Railway acquired Fenchurch Street Station as a second terminus when the Blackwall Railway was leased to the Great Eastern Company for 999 years. (The London Tilbury and Southend Railway also shared Fenchurch Street.)[8] The Great Eastern lines from Fenchurch Street ran through Leman Street and Shadwell Stations to a junction at Stepney where the line divided. "The right hand branch served the West India Docks and then Millwall, Poplar and Blackwall... The left hand branch ran through Burdett Road to link up with the Colchester main line at Bow."[9] Eventually Fenchurch Street was to provide a useful alternative for commuters from the suburban stations on the main line, and from the Loughton branch, as Fenchurch Street was nearer to their City destinations than Liverpool Street.

It was soon recognised that the Bishopsgate terminus was too small to deal with both goods and passenger traffic, and that it was placed in a fairly inaccessible location. The situation was summed up in a letter to shareholders, which was distributed in 1857:

"Your station (although conveniently situated for the North-Eastern corner of the City and suburbs) is most inconvenient and inaccessible for all other parts of the Metropolis, few omnibuses ply to it, and most of the approaches to it are so narrow that it is difficult to reach it, even in cabs, without serious delay. The station itself is very insufficient for the accommodation of the existing traffic, and so great confusion exists at busy hours of the day, that passengers accustomed to other lines are frequently heard expressing disgust and (what is of more consequence to you) they visit it as little as possible."[10]

In view of the shortcomings of Bishopsgate, the Great Eastern Company decided to build a new terminus, and consequently in 1864 a Bill was passed to allow work to proceed on a station to be called Liverpool Street.[11] The Great Eastern Railway Company was, however, in a poor financial position at this time. There was a need for additional capital to finance the project, but the borrowing powers of the company had already been exceeded. An investigation found that items that should have been charged to revenue had in fact been paid out of capital, and this finally resulted in an order being obtained at the Court of Chancery for the appointment of a receiver. A number of the company's creditors immediately claimed possession of the company's rolling stock, and plates were affixed to locomotives, stating that they belonged to certain creditors and were rented by them to the Great Eastern Railway Company. It was not until August 1867 that the financial crisis was relieved when the company obtained Parliamentary power to raise £3,000,000 by debenture stock, and this resulted in the preference shareholders and creditors agreeing to take the stock in settlement of their claims.[12]

The proposed construction site for Liverpool Street station was to cover ten acres of land, but before work could commence it was necessary for the Great Eastern Company to purchase properties that it had scheduled for demolition. However, it took a year-and-a-quarter for these demolitions to be completed in order to allow the contractor, Lucas Brothers, to commence work. Immediately to the west of Liverpool Street some demolition had already taken place as a result of the building of Broad Street station by the North London Railway. The building of these stations therefore altered a previously undesirable area and had the effect of moving the social problems of this part of the East End further eastwards:

> "The confusion of courts and alleys on their site had all the characteristics of an East End slum; houses subdivided and grossly overcrowded, mechanics living cheek by-jowl with costermongers, other casual labourers and those close to destitution."[13]

The new Liverpool Street station was completed by Lucas Brothers in two years, a feat that was achieved by working day and night during the second year. The contractor also supplied the thousands of bricks necessary for the construction work from their own brickyards near Lowestoft.[14] In order to achieve a link with the Metropolitan Railway at Bishopsgate, the new terminus was constructed at sub-street level. This necessitated a one in 70 incline starting at Bethnal Green and falling sufficiently to pass under Brick Lane. When Liverpool Street Station was opened on 1st November 1875, Bishopsgate Station ceased to deal with passenger traffic, thus enabling only goods traffic to be handled at the station.[15] In January 1879 an explosion occurred which shook the area, but fortunately there was no loss of life:

> "ALARMING EXPLOSION IN LONDON
> On Friday morning, about half-past eleven, the gas holder beneath the down platform of the Bishopsgate Station, on the Metropolitan Railway, exploded, causing considerable alarm, and shaking the houses in the neighbourhood. A bookstall was wrecked, but fortunately no one was injured. The traffic was not interrupted."[16]

It was noticed that the type of passenger arriving at Liverpool Street Station differed according to the time of arrival. The first workman's train came in at 5.25am:

> "...packed with none but working people; mostly men but some 'white-faced lads' and some women who take their turn of standing like the rest in the crowded compartments. After seven o'clock came the cheap trains bringing men and boys with a more contented and prosperous air and women who had a fresher and brighter look than their earlier sisters, wearing flowers and carrying novels and papers. As they finished arriving they were followed by the season ticket holders – clerks, professional and business men, and lady typists including first-class passengers. With later trains, in first class compartments, come the men who return again at four."[17]

Some of the early morning travellers arrived at Liverpool Street with time to spare before their work commenced. These people utilised the waiting-rooms, and some of them were in the habit of cooking red herrings for their breakfast. The smell caused by this practice caused the company to shut the waiting rooms, but they were subsequently re-opened for use by women workers only.[18]

The Great Eastern Railway Company soon realised that their new terminus was undersized to cope with an ever increasing volume of traffic, and consequently plans were made to extend the station eastwards. An Act for carrying out this work was obtained in 1887 and demolition work began in 1890. The contractor appointed to extend the station was John Mowlem and Company, and this firm commenced the construction work in 1892.[19]

> "When the enlargement was carried out the footbridge which ran across the western trainshed was extended into the new shed, providing a pedestrian route across the whole station with excellent views from it of all the goings-on below."[20]

A huge Gothic clock also hung in the main transept. It weighed two tons; the dials were 6ft in diameter; the case was 10ft square; and the height from pinnacle to base was 21ft.[2]

Work on the new eastern trainshed was finally completed in 1894. The completed station, however, was not entirely successful. The semi–underground location of the station magnified the noise from the steam engines, and smoke perpetually hung in the air. At the time of its completion, Liverpool Street station was the busiest terminus in London with continuous arrivals of suburban trains. The steam engines which caused much of the noise were Great Eastern 0-6-0 tank engines, which drew suburban services often made up of 17 four-wheeled coaches. By 1903 there were 416 daily arrivals at Liverpool Street.[22]

The Great Eastern Company also made alterations to its goods depot at Bishopsgate. The Italianate elevation of the original Shoreditch station was demolished, and a new façade 400ft long was constructed in a position nearer to the main street. The new goods depot was completed in August 1880 and had a covered area of 12 acres.

> "It is noteworthy that throughout the whole process of demolition and reconstruction goods traffic continued to be handled. Some 200–300 people were employed at this time, dealing with about 600 tons of goods each day. Fruit and vegetables from the Continent via Harwich was being received together with an amazing variety of manufactured goods... Up to 480 horse-drawn vans came and went during the day."[23]

# 14

## STRATFORD WORKS

In 1848 the Eastern Counties Railway moved locomotive maintenance work from its Romford Factory to a new site in Stratford, the Romford Factory being insufficient to cope with an increasing workload. The move was initiated by the soon to be disgraced Chairman of the ECR, the 'Railway King', George Hudson. Hudson also arranged for 300 houses to be built to accommodate the workers at the new Stratford Works, and the area quickly acquired the name 'Hudson's Town'. The new railway town was met with disapproval by some, as evidenced by a quotation from a local newspaper. "A city smokes where cornfields smiled before."[1]

The new Stratford Works were situated northwards of Stratford Station and were laid out to the west and east of what would eventually become the Great Eastern Main Line. In August 1850, John Viret Gooch became Locomotive Superintendent of the Eastern Counties Railway. Following a strike of ECR enginemen which had caused a great deal of trouble for the Company, Gooch took the important decision that in future the works should be used for both maintenance and engine construction. This resulted in the construction of the first 2-2-2T locomotive, which was given the number 20.

> "Overall Stratford Works built 1,702 locomotives, 5,500 passenger vehicles and 33,000 goods wagons (although a significant number of these were built at the nearby Temple Mills wagon works when wagon building moved from the Stratford site in 1896.)"[2]

In 1857 a major accident occurred when the fog signal factory set up at Stratford by the Eastern Counties Railway exploded, killing a Mr Beckwith who happened to be passing. A child had also been killed by an exploding ECR fog detonator in 1851. This apparent lack of safety led the Beckwith family to threaten legal action against the ECR, resulting in settlement of their claim for £1,000. A further claim of £250 was also settled by the railway company.[4]

When the Great Eastern Railway took over Stratford Works in 1862, work on the construction and maintenance of locomotives increased, and between 1870 and 1900 a total of 960 locomotives were completed. It also became one of the first UK railway companies to build omnibuses in its own workshops at Stratford.[3]

> "A time record for the building of a locomotive was eventually set at Stratford Works in 1891 when a tender engine was built in nine hours and 47 minutes from the time that the frames were stamped out to the completed and fully functional locomotive leaving the works. This record still stands."[5]

The training of apprentices was considered important by both the ECR and the GER, and consequently a thriving training scheme was developed, which lasted until closure of the works in 1963. Apprentices were allowed to attend colleges on day release, and a typical apprentice would then gain experience by working in the various repair and maintenance shops. During a five-year training period an apprentice might work in the Tool Shop, the Fitting Shop, the Westinghouse Shop, the Erecting Shop, and in the Production Office.[6] He would then be recognised as a fully trained fitter.

When Stratford Works first opened it employed over 1,000 people, but by 1912 this figure had risen to 6,500. These people were fully occupied on work for the Great Eastern Railway. However, additional duties had to be undertaken during World War I when munitions work was carried out at Stratford and a hospital train was constructed for the army. Grouping in 1923 brought the Great Eastern Railway to an end, but the Stratford Works continued to maintain GER locomotives, many of which ran until the steam era ended in the 1960s.

The Locomotive Superintendents employed by the Great Eastern Railway rarely stayed at the Stratford Works for lengthy periods. After moving on, some became distinguished locomotive engineers with other railway companies:

"Among these in particular was Samuel W. Johnson, who served from 1866 until he left to become Locomotive Superintendent of the Midland Railway in 1873; W. Adams, who succeeded him but resigned in 1878 to take up a corresponding appointment on the London & South Western Railway; and T. W. Worsdell, who took office in 1881 but left for the North Eastern Railway in 1885. The founder of the well-known locomotive building firm of Kitson of Leeds, William Kitson, also was Locomotive Superintendent of the Great Eastern Railway for a year, between 1865 and 1866."[7]

The entrepreneurial spirit also flourished at Stratford. One enterprising fitter arranged for a farmer friend to shoot rabbits, which were then crated and dispatched to Stratford Works by train so that they could be sold to the workers. The farmer was extremely proficient with a shot gun, and paid 1d per cartridge, but the rabbits sold for between 10d and 1 shilling, depending on their size.[8]

# Appendix 1

### Eastern Union Railway.

## CHRISTMAS DAY.

ON CHRISTMAS DAY, the TRAINS will leave BISHOPGATE STATION, LONDON, as on Sundays, at 8 0 a.m., and 6 0 p.m., for IPSWICH, BURY, and NORWICH, arriving at the latter Station at 2 0 and 11 30 p.m. Trains will leave the

### Victoria Station, Norwich,

At 6 20 a.m., and 2 10 p.m., for London and intermediate Stations, arriving in London at 2 15 and 9 45 p.m.

### A LOCAL TRAIN

Will leave COLCHESTER for IPSWICH, BURY, and NORWICH, at 7 30 a.m.; and from NORWICH for BURY, IPSWICH, and COLCHESTER, at 5 30 p.m. as usual, calling at all the Stations.

### RETURN TICKETS

Taken at any of the Stations on the 24th or 25th will be available up to, and including the 26th December.

Norfolk Chronicle 22/12/1849

Within three years of its opening in 1846 the Eastern Union Railway ran a comprehensive Christmas service into London.

# Appendix 2

The following abridged article concerning the new Liverpool Street Station appeared in the *Ipswich Journal* on Tuesday 26th October 1875.

### THE NEW GREAT EASTERN TERMINUS IN LONDON

The finishing touches are now being applied to that vast pile of buildings which are henceforth to serve as the terminus in London of the Great Eastern Railway, and by Saturday next, or at the latest Monday, passengers to and from East Anglia will alight at, or depart from, the largest and in many respects the best and most convenient Railway Station in London, instead of, as hitherto, the smallest and most inconvenient. The completion of this great work inaugurates a new era in the history of the Company. The opening of the Liverpool Street Station marks the entire completion of that of Metropolitan extensions which has so seriously impeded its welfare for the last ten years, and in which it has expended some six millions of capital. It is also the means of opening up communication with the entire railway system of the country and the Metropolis both North and South of the Thames. The importance of this event to the Company can scarcely be over estimated. For many years the old Station at Shoreditch has been altogether inadequate to the requirements of the line. Built as the original terminus of the Eastern Counties Railway, in its first conception, be it remembered but a mere by-way or branch, it has remained as the terminus of the entire Great Eastern system, notwithstanding that the line which it serves has become the fifth longest in the British Isles. Line after line has been added to the system, but, owing to its crowded surroundings, a wing was never added to the Station till, when the Company undertook to work the Tilbury and Southend and Woolwich Lines, they were compelled to erect the unsightly and avowedly only temporary sheds which stand on its Northern side.

The journey from Bishopsgate Station from anywhere West of Temple

Bar or South of London Bridge, has not inaptly been termed a day's march, and many indeed must be those who have taken as long in getting from Charing Cross to the station as it has taken them to accomplish the entire journey by rail. All this is now to be altered, and after next Monday arriving passengers in London will have to rub their eyes and look around them to assure themselves they are not dreaming, if they be not warned beforehand of what they are to expect... The Station buildings proper (not including the enormous iron and glass roof) form an L-shaped block, the apex of the latter running at right angles with Liverpool Street, and the tail extending to the Broad Street Station, the space between the two points of the L being the station yard for the arrival platform... Messrs Smith & Son will have two very large and convenient bookstalls, one at the main line departure platform, and one in the open space under the transept fronting the suburban platforms. The lavatories and sanitary conveniences are on the most approved principles, and are contained in picturesque looking buildings, erected on each platform away from the main station buildings. The exterior of the building is of London stock brick, with Bath stone dressings, whilst inside the work is carefully pointed, and the yellow of the stock bricks plentifully relieved with red bricks and Bath stone... The iron and wood work is painted brown, whilst the columns and roof are a dark green... The works were designed by Mr Wilson, the Company's engineer, and, as above stated the contractors were Messrs Lucas Brothers.

# Appendix 3

## A Great Eastern Railway Pension Fund Certificate

# Appendix 4

Report of an accident that took place on the Eastern Counties Railway on 4th August 1845.

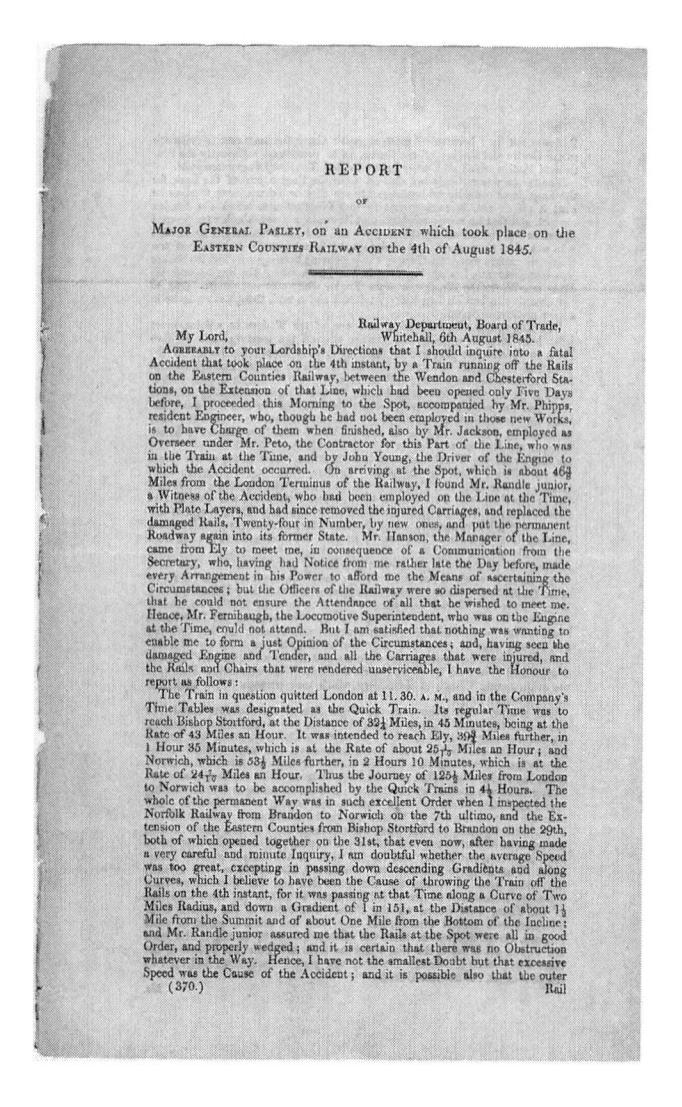

## REPORT

OF

Major General Pasley, on an Accident which took place on the Eastern Counties Railway on the 4th of August 1845.

Railway Department, Board of Trade,
My Lord,   Whitehall, 6th August 1845.

Agreeably to your Lordship's Directions that I should inquire into a fatal Accident that took place on the 4th instant, by a Train running off the Rails on the Eastern Counties Railway, between the Wendon and Chesterford Stations, on the Extension of that Line, which had been opened only Five Days before, I proceeded this Morning to the Spot, accompanied by Mr. Phipps, resident Engineer, who, though he had not been employed in those new Works, is to have Charge of them when finished, also by Mr. Jackson, employed as Overseer under Mr. Peto, the Contractor for this Part of the Line, who was in the Train at the Time, and by John Young, the Driver of the Engine to which the Accident occurred. On arriving at the Spot, which is about 46¾ Miles from the London Terminus of the Railway, I found Mr. Randle junior, a Witness of the Accident, who had been employed on the Line at the Time, with Plate Layers, and had since removed the injured Carriages, and replaced the damaged Rails, Twenty-four in Number, by new ones, and put the permanent Roadway again into its former State. Mr. Hanson, the Manager of the Line, came from Ely to meet me, in consequence of a Communication from the Secretary, who, having had Notice from me rather late the Day before, made every Arrangement in his Power to afford me the Means of ascertaining the Circumstances; but the Officers of the Railway were so dispersed at the Time, that he could not ensure the Attendance of all that he wished to meet me. Hence, Mr. Fernihaugh, the Locomotive Superintendent, who was on the Engine at the Time, could not attend. But I am satisfied that nothing was wanting to enable me to form a just Opinion of the Circumstances; and, having seen the damaged Engine and Tender, and all the Carriages that were injured, and the Rails and Chairs that were rendered unserviceable, I have the Honour to report as follows:

The Train in question quitted London at 11.30. A. M., and in the Company's Time Tables was designated as the Quick Train. Its regular Time was to reach Bishop Stortford, at the Distance of 32¼ Miles, in 45 Minutes, being at the Rate of 43 Miles an Hour. It was intended to reach Ely, 39¾ Miles further, in 1 Hour 35 Minutes, which is at the Rate of about 25 1/13 Miles an Hour; and Norwich, which is 53½ Miles further, in 2 Hours 10 Minutes, which is at the Rate of 24 7/10 Miles an Hour. Thus the Journey of 125½ Miles from London to Norwich was to be accomplished by the Quick Trains in 4½ Hours. The whole of the permanent Way was in such excellent Order when I inspected the Norfolk Railway from Brandon to Norwich on the 7th ultimo, and the Extension of the Eastern Counties from Bishop Stortford to Brandon on the 29th, both of which opened together on the 31st, that even now, after having made a very careful and minute Inquiry, I am doubtful whether the average Speed was too great, excepting in passing down descending Gradients and along Curves, which I believe to have been the Cause of throwing the Train off the Rails on the 4th instant, for it was passing at that Time along a Curve of Two Miles Radius, and down a Gradient of 1 in 151, at the Distance of about 1¼ Mile from the Summit and of about One Mile from the Bottom of the Incline; and Mr. Randle junior assured me that the Rails at the Spot were all in good Order, and properly wedged; and it is certain that there was no Obstruction whatever in the Way. Hence, I have not the smallest Doubt but that excessive Speed was the Cause of the Accident; and it is possible also that the outer

(370.)   Rail

( 2 )

Rail may not have been raised quite so much above the inner one, in reference to the Centre and Radius of the Curve, as to counteract sufficiently the centrifugal Motion which all Curves have a natural Tendency to communicate.

The Steam was certainly shut off when the Engine ran off the Line, for the Enginemen candidly acknowledged to me that he did not know whether he shut it off or not, in consequence of that Circumstance, before the Engine overset, and that he was so confused that he could not say whether he jumped down, or was thrown off by the Shock. He, and Mr. Fernihaugh, his Officer, who was also thrown off, and said to have found himself under one of the Carriages, made a wonderful Escape, neither having been injured; but the Stoker was less fortunate, having been crushed to Death under the Engine, and his Body burned, for the Woodwork of the Engine afterwards caught fire. One of the Guards also had his Leg badly fractured, and is said, though alive, to be in a very precarious State.

The Engineman was of opinion that one of the Wedges at a Joint must have been loose or wanting, and thereby allowed the meeting Rails of Two Rails to separate, so that one of them must have struck the Flange of the Wheel of his Engine, and thrown it off. Mr. Randle junior declared, that all the Wedges were firmly fixed, and on inspecting the first injured Rail, Part of the Flange of which had been broken by the Wheel on running off, this Assertion was proved to be true, because the Piece of the Rail that was splintered was not entirely separated when I examined it, and must evidently have been split by a downward Blow, so that the Wheel must have jumped up before it struck the End of the Rail in this violent Manner. Mr. Jackson informed me that he felt the Wheel jump, and heard it strike. The Order of the Train was as follows: First, the Engine and Tender; secondly, the Luggage Van; thirdly, a Horse Box, with Two Horses in it; fourthly, the Passenger Carriages, Six in Number, (viz. Two Second Class, Three First Class, and One Second Class Carriage,) followed by a Gentleman's Carriage on a Truck in rear of all. As soon as the Train was stopped by the overseting of the Engine, Mr. Jackson, who had been in a First Class Coupé, assisted the Passengers to get out from the Two leading Second Class Carriages, the Roofs of which were burning in consequence of the Luggage above them having caught fire. He then went to the Horse Box, which was also burning; and as the Door was blocked up, he made the Railway Labourers present beat in one End with their Pickaxes, which being removed the Horses were got out very little injured. Neither Mr. Randle junior nor Mr. Jackson, who were equally active in assisting the Passengers, could inform me whether any of them were seriously injured, but they believed not, because none of them remained above an Hour or two at the Inn at Chesterford, to which they were conveyed in the first instance. A Coroner's Inquest is appointed to be held To-morrow upon the Body of the unfortunate Stoker, at the neighbouring Village of Littlebury, which may perhaps throw additional Light upon the Subject.

The Engine, which overset on the Right Side of the Railway, about 103 Yards from the Point where it quitted the Rails, was slewed round on striking the Embankment with its far End, so that the Chimney, which was broken by the Shock, was turned round towards London. In other respects it was little injured, excepting that the Life Guards or Irons in front, which nearly touch the Rails, were broken off, the Foot Plate on which the Engineman and Stoker stood was doubled up and broken; and the Cleading or Wooden Casing round the Boiler, which has been burned, will require to be replaced. The Carriage or lower Part of the Tender was turned upside down, with its Wheels in Air, little injured; but the Tank was separated from it, and much broken, having been overset on the Left Side of the Cutting; Sir, as usually happens on such Occasions, the Tender and Engine went off the Rails in contrary Directions. The Luggage Van also was overturned, but otherwise little injured, not having been set on fire, like the Horse Box and the Two Second Class Carriages immediately in rear of it; but these, as well as the other Carriages of the Train, were forced off the Rails. The Roofs of the Second Class Carriages were burned through, but they were not much damaged in other respects, except that one of them was shattered, more by turning it over upon the Top to get it out of the Way; and the Axle and Two hind Wheels of the other were broken off, though the Body was perfect, except one End, split by the Seat of the unfortunate Guard.

Mr.

( 3 )

Mr. Bulkeley, the Secretary, informed me, that the Directors of the Railway Company would make any Change in their Arrangements that the Lords of the Committee of Privy Council for Trade might be pleased to recommend. I beg leave, therefore, to submit to your Lordship's Consideration, that this Accident appears to have been proved in regard to a very perfect new Line, what has often been proved before in respect to less perfect ones, namely, that it is best to cause the Passenger Trains to move with very moderate Velocity after the opening of a Railway, until the permanent Road shall be consolidated by Time, and by the continual Labour and Attention of the Plate Layers and of the Persons superintending them; for your Lordship knows that an alarming Accident on the Great Western, and one on the Edinburgh and Glasgow Railway, the latter attended with Loss of Life, both took place after adopting the System of Express Trains, in consequence of those Trains moving with increased Velocity over Parts of those respective Lines that had been passed with Safety for Years before by their ordinary Trains. A slight Degree of Elasticity or longitudinal Sleepers, or a very trifling Difference of level of transverse Sleepers, may throw an Engine or Carriage off the Rails, at a high Rate of Velocity, which would not produce any such injurious Effect at a more moderate Speed.

Hence I beg leave to suggest, that the Eastern Counties Railway Company be requested to order the Speed of their quickest Trains on the new Part of their Line, and the Norfolk Railway Company on their whole Line, to be reduced to a Time from an Average of about 25 to not exceeding 20 Miles an Hour, and to caution their Enginemen to slacken their Speed along Curves and on descending Gradients. The former can always be distinguished by the Eye, but not the latter; therefore it is desirable that they should also adopt the System of making known every Change of Gradient, by acting up a Post and a Couple of Arms, on either which the Word "Level" to denote a horizontal Plane, or the Rate of Inclination, such as 1 in 100, 1 in 150, &c. &c., should be marked conspicuously, as has been done on the London and Birmingham, Midland Counties, and other Railways, and that the Length of the Plane should also be marked, as on the London and Croydon Railway, where this sort of Notation is the clearest of any that I have seen. It is true that experienced Enginemen on any Railway know the Gradients, which they learn by Degrees without such Marks; but they are so useful to new Enginemen, and also so satisfactory to Passengers, that I think they ought to be general on all Railways.

I have, &c.
(Signed) C. W. PASLEY, Major General,
Inspector General of Railways.

The Right Hon.
The Earl of Dalhousie.

P.S.— Mr. Phipps informed me, that the Tender of one of the Up Trains going at moderate Speed on the 1st instant went off the Rails near Elsenham, about 37¼ Miles from London, on the new Part of the Eastern Counties Railway, owing to very slight Subsidence, by which the Train was delayed Two Hours. This Fact, combined with several other similar Cases that I have known within the last Two Years to occur at or soon after the opening of new Lines, though none but that which formed the Subject of the foregoing Letter proved fatal, strongly corroborates the Necessity of commencing with a moderate Speed on all new Lines or Extensions.

# Notes

**THE RAILWAY NAVVIES**
1. Evans, Eric. J., *The Forging of the Modern State*, p.132–133
2. *Cassell's History of England,* Vol V, p.191
3. Coleman, Terry, *The Railway Navvies*, p.25
4. *The Ipswich Journal,* 23rd August 1862
5. Coleman, Terry, *The Railway Navvies,* p.108–109
6. Helps, Arthur, *The Life and Labours of Mr Brassey,* p.327
7. Helps, Arthur, *The Life and Labours of Mr Brassey*, p.45–46
8. Norrie, Charles M., *Bridging the Years – A Short History of British Civil Engineering*, p.92
9. Joby, R. S., *The Railway Builders*, p.xx
10. Brodribb, John, *An Illustrated History of the East Suffolk Railway*, p.23
11. *The Bury & Norwich Post,* 19th February 1849
12. Parliamentary Papers 1846 – Report of Select Committee on Railway labourers, p.iii
13. Parliamentary Papers 1846, Vol 4 Q.2523
14. Parliamentary Papers 1846, Vol 4 Q.1363
15. Moffat, Hugh, *East Anglia's First Railways*, p.35
16. *The Bury & Norwich Post,* 24th April 1850
17. Ipswich Records Office (HA1/HB6/3/29), 26th December 1845
18. *The Ipswich Journal,* 16th November 1850
19. *The Ipswich Journal,* 18th August 1849
20. Moffat, Hugh, *East Anglia's First Railways*, p.184/185

**EARLY EAST ANGLIAN STATIONS**
1. Paar & Gray, *The Life and Times of teat Eastern Railway*, p.85
1A. *Wolverton Station Museum*
1B. Biddle, Gordon, *Victorian Stations*, p.42
2. *Our Transport Heritage* website

3   Biddle, Gordon, *Victorian Stations*, p.113/114
4   Comfort, N. A., *The Mid-Suffolk Light Railway*, p.18
5   Comfort, N. A., *The Mid-Suffolk Light Railway*, p.27
6   Gordon, D. I., *The Eastern Counties,* Vol 5, p.190
7   *Ipswich Journal*, 24/02/1885
8   Hawkings, David T., *Railway Ancestors*, p.16
9   Joby, R. S., *The Railwaymen*, p.29
10  *Ipswich Journal*, 29/05/1858
11  Joby, R. S., *The Railwaymen*, p.27
12  *Ipswich Journal*, 17/02/1855
13  *Ipswich Journal*, 06/02/1847
14  Paar, H. W., *Loughton's First Railway Station*, p.5
15  *Ipswich Journal*, 03/10/1900
16  Moffat, H., *East Anglia's First Railways*, p.99/101
17  Paar, H. W., *Loughton's First Railway Station*, p.23
18  *The Penny Illustrated Paper*, 30/04/1898, p.282
19  Comfort, N. A., *The Mid-Suffolk Light Railway*, p.99
20  *Internet*, myweb.tiscali.co.uk/coal
21  *Ipswich Journal*, 10/07/1875

## ENGINE DRIVERS AND GUARDS

1   Gordon, D. I., *The Eastern Counties*, Vol 5, p.31
2   *East Anglian Magazine*, December 1973, p.88
3   Hawkings, David. T., *Railway Ancestors*, RAIL 186/100, p.32
3A  May, Trevor, *The Victorian Railway Worker*, p.14
4   Moffat, Hugh, *East Anglia's First Railways*, p.104 & 216/17
5   *East Anglian Magazine*, December 1973, p.90
6   Ransom, P. J. G., *The Victorian Railway*, p.149
7   Rolt, L. T. C., *Red For Danger*, p.120
8   *Ipswich Journal*, 13/09/1847
9   Summers, A., *Accidents on the Great Eastern*, No. 23
10  *Ipswich Journal*, 25/02/1882
11  *The Graphic*, 16/12/1882
12  *Ipswich Journal*, 14/11/1863
13  *East Anglian Magazine*, December 1973, p.90
14  *The Penny Illustrated Paper*, 11/02/1865, p.91
15  *Ipswich Journal*, 07/02/1846

## FREIGHT

1. Gale, J., *Transport in Suffolk in the Coaching Era*
2. Moffat, Hugh, *East Anglia's First Railways*, p.70
3. Moffat, Hugh, *East Anglia's First Railways*, p.108
4. *Goods & Not So Goods (Freight Operations)* Internet
4A. Simmons, Jack, *The Railways of Britain*, p.225
5. Kingsford, P. W., *Victorian Railwaymen*, p.37
6. Conveyance Note, *Eastern Union Railway Company*, October 1851
7. *Ipswich Journal*, 11/02/1860
8. Barney, John, *The Norfolk Railway*, p.105
9. Barney, John, *The Norfolk Railway*, p.112
10. *The Penny Illustrated Paper*, 26/04/1862
11. Joby, R. S., *East Anglia*, p.9/10
12. Gordon, D. I., *The Eastern Counties*, Vol 5, p.31
13. *Ipswich Journal*, 04/12/1847
14. *The Graphic*, 01/02/1896
15. Paye, Peter, *The Snape Branch*, p.65
16. Gordon, D. I., *The Eastern Counties*, Vol 5, p.81/82

## SIGNALLING

1. *Eastern Counties Railway – Signals and Regulations*, 20/12/1846
2. *Great Eastern Railway Magazine*, April 1914, p.114/15
3. Webster, H. C., *Railways for All*, p.126/27
4. Moffat, Hugh, *East Anglia's First Railways*, p.96
5. *Ipswich Journal*, 24/03/1866
6. *Great Eastern Railway Magazine*, April 1914, p.114
7. Webster, H. C., *Railways for All*, p.127
8. *The Railway Magazine*, August 1962, p.523
9. *Ipswich Journal*, 10/09/1864
10. *Ipswich Journal*, 07/01/1865
11. *Ipswich Journal*, 27/02/1888
12. *Ipswich Journal*, 27/04/1872 & 03/08/1875
13. *The Graphic*, 22/11/1890
14. *Great Eastern Railway Magazine*, June 1914, p.199
15. *Great Eastern Railway Magazine*, June 1913, p.203

## PLATELAYERS

1. Moffat, Hugh, *East Anglia's First Railways*, p.123/124/125
2. Webster, H. C., *Railways for All*, p.189/90
3/4/5. *Eastern Counties Railway,* Signals and Regulations, 20/12/1846
6. *Ipswich Journal*, 21/09/1850
7. Ransom, P. J. G., *The Victorian Railway*, p.99
8. *Eastern Counties Railway,* Signals and Regulations, 20/12/1846
9. Moffat, Hugh, *East Anglia's First Railways*, p.126
10. Rolt, L. T. C., *Red For Danger*, p.130/131/132
11/12. *The Penny Illustrated Paper and Illustrated Times*, 30/09/1905
13. *Eastern Counties Railway,* Signals and Regulations, 20/12/1846
14. Kingsford, P. W., *Victorian Railwaymen*, p.138
15. *Great Eastern Railway Magazine*, March 1914, p.100
16. Kingsford, P. W., *Victorian Railwaymen*, p.99/100
17. *Eastern Counties Railway,* Signals and Regulations, 20/12/1846
18. Great Eastern Railway memorandum, 19/08/1886
19. *Ipswich Journal*, 14/06/1851
20. *Ipswich Journal*, 23/05/1871

## HOTELS AND SEASIDE HOLIDAYS

1. Ransom, P. J. G., *The Victorian Railway*, p.89
2. *British Railway Journal* (Special Great Eastern Edition), p.72
3. *British Railway Journal* (Special Great Eastern Edition), p.73
4. Hannavy, John, *The English Seaside in Victorian and Edwardian Times*, p.6
5. *The Graphic*, 22/09/1877
6. Hannavy, John, *The English Seaside in Victorian and Edwardian Times*, p.109
7. *The Penny Illustrated Paper*, 15/04/1871
8. *The Penny Illustrated Paper and Illustrated Times*, 12/08/1876
9. *The Penny Illustrated Paper and Illustrated Times*, 05/09/1874
10. Simmons, Jack, *The Railways of Britain*, p.203
11. *The Graphic*, 16/08/1873
12. *The Graphic*, 05/09/1874
13. *Scenes from a Signalbox,* A social history of Britain's railways, p.154
14. Walsh, B. D. J., *The Railway Magazine*, August 1962, p.527

15 Gordon, D. I., *The Eastern Counties*, Vol 5, p.78
16 *The Penny Illustrated Paper and Illustrated Times*, 16/04/1881
17 Gordon, D. I., *The Eastern Counties*, Vol 5, p.75
18 *Scenes from a Signalbox,* A social history of Britain's railways, p.152
19 *The Railway Magazine*, June 1904

**ACCIDENTS**
1 Kingsford, P. W., *Victorian Railwaymen*, p.47
2 *The Penny Illustrated Paper*, 17/05/1862
3 Fairburn, Sir William, *Reports of Railway Benevolent Institution*, 1865
4 Gordon, D. I., *The Eastern Counties*, Vol 5, p.31
5 *Ipswich Journal*, 19/01/1856
6 Hilton, H. F., *The Eastern Union Railway*, p.37
7 *Ipswich Journal*, 19/09/1846
8 *Ipswich Journal*, 13/01/1855
9 *Ipswich Journal*, 14/01/1854
10 Rolt, L. T. C., *Red For Danger*, p.76
11 *The Penny Illustrated Paper*, 01/09/186
12 *Ipswich Journal*, 19/10/1872
13 *The Penny Illustrated Paper and Illustrated Times*, 19/09/1874
14 Rolt, L. T. C., *Red For Danger*, p.143/146
14A *The Railway Magazine*, October 1907
15 Hewison, C. H., *Locomotive Boiler Explosions*, p.45
16 Hewison, C. H., *Locomotive Boiler Explosions*, p.59
17 Hewison, C. H., *Locomotive Boiler Explosions*, p.35
18 *Ipswich Journal*, 11/05/186
19/20 Board of Trade (Railway Department), 13/11/1900
21 Hewison, C. H., *Locomotive Boiler Explosions*, p.108/109
22 Board of Trade (Railway Department), 13/11/1900
23 *The Graphic*, 18/04/1896

**CARRIAGES AND LOCOMOTIVES**
1 *Great Eastern Railway Magazine*, October 1913, p.334
2 Ransom, P. J. G., *The Victorian Railway*, p.180
3 Hilton, H. F., *The Eastern Union Railway*, Appendix C

4 Moffat, Hugh, *East Anglia's First Railways*, p.112/114
5 *The Railway Magazine*, August 1962, p.519
6 *The Locomotive Magazine*, 1905
7 *Great Eastern Railway Magazine*, June 1914, p.175
8 *The Penny Illustrated Paper*, 09/05/1863
9 *Ipswich Journal*, 27/03/1877
10 *The Railway Magazine*, August 1962, p.523
11 Swinger, Peter, *W. East Anglia*, p.10
12 *The Railway Magazine*, August 1962, p.527
13 Ransom, P. J. G., *The Victorian Railway*, p.80
14 Ransom, P. J. G., *The Victorian Railway*, p.80/81
15 Hamilton Ellis, *19th Century Railway Carriages*, p.36
16 Hamilton Ellis, *19th Century Railway Carriages*, p.29
17 *Great Eastern Railway Magazine*, June 1913, p.180
18 Hamilton Ellis, *19th Century Railway Carriages*, p.60
19 *The Graphic*, 29/04/1871
20/21 Moffat, Hugh, *East Anglia's First Railways*, p.118
22 *Great Eastern Railway Magazine*, June 1914, p.174
23 *Ipswich Journal*, 02/09/1879
24 Smith, Gavin, *The Great Eastern Railway*, p.44

## PASSENGERS
1 Smith, David. Norman, *The Railway and Its Passengers*, p.12
2 Quinn, T., *Tales of the Old Railwaymen*, p.70
3 Smith, David Norman, *The Railway and Its Passengers*, p.19
4 *Norfolk News*, 18/10/1865
5 Smith, David Norman, *The Railway and Its Passengers*, p.102
6 Smith, David Norman, *The Railway and Its Passengers*, p.105
7 *Great Eastern Railway Magazine*, May 1913, p.146
8/9 *The Graphic*, 04/05/1878
10 Farmer, Jack, *The Great Eastern Railway As I Knew It*, p.125
11 Smith, David Norman, *The Railway and Its Passengers*, p.106
12 *Great Eastern Railway Magazine*, June 1914, p.187

## LEVEL CROSSINGS
1 Brodribb, John, *An Illustrated History of the East Suffolk Railway*, p.228

2 *Ipswich Journal*, 25/06/1870
3 *Ipswich Journal*, 17/11/1883
4 Barking & Dagenham Local Studies Library
5 *Lowestoft Weekly Journal*, Nov. 1874
6 *The York Herald*, 22/10/1874
7 *The Newsman*, 17/10/1885
8 Kingsford, P. W., *Victorian Railwaymen*, p.94
9 Kingsford, P. W., *Victorian Railwaymen*, p.155
10 *Great Eastern Railway Magazine*, June 1914, p.199
11 *Great Eastern Railway Magazine*, June 1913, p.204

## INDUSTRIAL RELATIONS
1 Kingsford, P. W., *Victorian Railwaymen*, p.13/15
2 Kingsford, P. W., *Victorian Railwaymen*, p.17/18
3 *Great Eastern Railway Magazine*, June 1913, p.180
4 *Ipswich Journal*, 17/08/1850
5 *Ipswich Journal*, 24/08/1850
6 Kingsford, P. W., *Victorian Railwaymen*, p.78
7 Kingsford, P. W., *Victorian Railwaymen*, p.81
8 *Ipswich Journal*, 24/08/1850
9 *Ipswich Journal*, 24/08/1850
10 Kingsford, P. W., *Victorian Railwaymen*, p.32 & 81
11 Moffat, Hugh, *East Anglia's First Railways*, p.39/40
12 Kingsford, P. W., *Victorian Railwaymen*, p.73
13 Internet – unionancestors.co.uk
14 *Great Eastern Railway Magazine*, May 1913, p.171 & April 1914, p.132
15 Kingsford, P. W., *Victorian Railwaymen*, Appendix 1
16 Roodenburg, H., *Social Control in Europe*, p.86
17 GER Pension & Superannuation Certificate, No. 2563
18 GER Accident Fund – Scheme and Rules
19 *Prevention of Accidents to Staff Engaged in Railway Operation*, p.3

## THE LONDON TERMINI
1 Moffat, Hugh, *East Anglia's First Railways*, p.12/14
2 *Devonshire Street Railway Station*, Internet *Wikipedia*
3 *Ipswich Journal*, 26/10/1875

4   Biddle, Gordon, *Victorian Stations*, p.34
5   *Norfolk Chronicle*, 02/08/1862
6   *British Railway Journal* (Special Great Eastern Edition), p.80/85
7   *British Railway Journal* (Special Great Eastern Edition), p.87
8   Smith, Gavin, *The Great Eastern Railway*, p.120
9   *British Railway Journal* (Special Great Eastern Edition), p.51
10  *Liverpool Street Station*, Greater London Council, p.15
11  *Liverpool Street Station*, Greater London Council, p.20
12  *The Railway Magazine*, August 1962, p.521/523
13/14 *Liverpool Street Station*, Greater London Council, p.27/28
15  *British Railway Journal* (Special Great Eastern Edition), p.91
16  *The Dundee Courier*, 21/01/1879
17/18 *Liverpool Street Station*, Greater London Council, p.47
19/20 *Liverpool Street Station*, Greater London Council, p.31/32
21  *Great Eastern Railway Magazine*, June 1914, p.188
22  *Liverpool Street Station*, Greater London Council, p.52
23  *British Railway Journal* (Special Great Eastern Edition), p.92

## STRATFORD WORKS
1   Allen, Cecil. J., *The Great Eastern Railway*, p.17/18
2/3 *Wikipedia*
4   Paar & Gray, *The Life & Times of the Great Eastern Railway*, p.20/21
5   Smith, Robert, 'A Moment of Glory', *Great Eastern Journal*, Jan. 1992
6   Hammond, L. G., *Stratford Locomotive Works Recalled*, p.iii
7   Allen, Cecil. J., *The Great Eastern Railway*, p.84
8   Paar & Gray, *The Life & Times of the Great Eastern Railway*, p.46

# Bibliography

1 Allen, Cecil. J., *The Great Eastern Railway*, Ian Allen Ltd, 1955
1A Barney, John, *The Norfolk Railway*, Mintaka Books, 2007
2 Biddle, Gordon, *Victorian Stations*, David & Charles, 1973
3 Brodribb, John, *The East Suffolk Railway*, Ian Allen Publishing Ltd, 2003
4 *Cassell's History of England*, London; Cassell & Company Ltd
5 Coleman, Terry, *The Railway Navvies*, Penguin Books Ltd, 1968
6 Comfort, N. A., *The Mid-Suffolk Light Railway*, The Oakwood Press, 1963
7 Evans, Eric. J., *The Forging of the Modern State*, New York; Longman, 1983
8 Greater London Council, *Liverpool Street Station*, Academy Editions, 1978
9 Gale, J., *Transport in Suffolk in the Coaching Era*, Await Publication
10 Farmer, J., *The Great Eastern Railway As I Knew It*, Woodgrange Press, 1990
11 Gordon, D. I., *The Eastern Counties* Vol 5, David & Charles, 1968
12 Hamilton Ellis, *19th Century Railway Carriages*, Modern Transport, 1949
12A Hammond, L. G., *BR Eastern Region Stratford Locomotive Works Recalled*
13 Hannavy, John, *The English Seaside in Victorian & Edwardian Times*, Shire Library, 2003
14 Hawkings, David T., *Railway Ancestors*, The History Press Ltd, 1995
15 Helps, Arthur, *The Life and Labours of Mr Brassey*, Evelyn Adams & Mackay Ltd, 1872
16 Hewison, C. H., *Locomotive Boiler Explosions*, David & Charles, 1983
17 Hilton, H. F., *The Eastern Union Railway*, The London & North Eastern Railway, 1946
18 Joby, R. S., *The Railway Builders*, David & Charles, 1983

19 Joby, R. S., *The Railwaymen*, David & Charles, 1984
20 Joby, R. S., *East Anglia*, David & Charles, 1977
21 Kingsford, P. W., *Victorian Railwaymen*, Frank Cass & Co. Ltd, 1970
22 May, Trevor, *The Victorian Railway Worker*, Shire Publications, 2003
23 Moffat, Hugh, *East Anglia's First Railways*, Terence Dalton Ltd, 1987
24 Norrie, Charles, *A Short History of British Civil Engineering*, Edward Arnold Ltd, 1956
25 Parr, H. W., *Loughton's First Railway Station*, Loughton & District Historical Society, 1996
26 Paar & Gray, *The Life & Times of the Great Eastern Railway*, Castlemead Publications, 1991
27 Paye, Peter, *The Snape Branch*, The Oakwood Press, 2005
28 Quinn, Tom, *Tales of the Old Railwaymen*, David & Charles, 1998
29 Ransom, P. J. G., *The Victorian Railway*, William Heinemann Ltd, 1990
30 Rolt, L. T. C., *Red For Danger*, David & Charles, 1955
31 Roodenburg, Herman, *Social Control in Europe*, Google Books
32 *Scenes From a Signal Box,* A social history of Britain's railways, David & Charles, 2001
33 Simmons, Jack, *The Railways of Britain*, Sheldrake Publishing, 1986
34 Smith, Gavin, *The Great Eastern Railway*, Tempus Publishing Ltd, 1996
35 Smith, David Norman, *The Railway and Its Passengers*, David & Charles, 1988
36 Summers, Alan, *Accidents on the Great Eastern* (on sale at the former Wells Station)
37 Swinger, Peter: W., *East Anglia*, David & Charles, 1983
38 Webster, H. C., *Railways For All*, Ward, Lock & Co, 1950

## PRIMARY SOURCES
1 Board of Trade (Railway Department) 13/11/1900
2 Conveyance Note - Eastern Union Railway Company (October 1851)
3 Fairburn, Sir William, *Reports of Railway Benevolent Institution*, 1865
4 Great Eastern Railway Accident Fund – Scheme & Rules, 1919

5 Great Eastern Railway Pension & Superannuation Certificate No. 2563
6 Ipswich Records Office, *Proposed railways from Stowmarket*, HA1/HB6/3/29 (26/12/1845)
7 Memorandum – Great Eastern Railway, 19/08/1886
8 Parliamentary Papers 1846, *Report of Select Committee on Railway Labourers*
9 Parliamentary Papers 1846, Vol 4, Q.2523
10 Parliamentary Papers 1846, Vol 4, Q.1363
11 *Prevention of Accidents to Staff Engaged in Railway Operations*, Published BY GWR, LNER, LMS, and SR
12 *Signals & Regulations*, Eastern Counties Railway, 20/12/1846

## NEWSPAPERS
1 *Bury & Norwich Post*
2 *Dundee Courier*
3 *The Graphic*
4 *Ipswich Journal*
5 *The Newsman*
6 *Norfolk Chronicle*
7 *Norfolk News*
8 *The Penny Illustrated Paper*
9 *York Herald*

## PERIODICALS
1 *British Railways Journal* (Special Great Eastern Edition)
2 *East Anglia Magazine*
3 *Great Eastern Railway Magazine*
4 *The Locomotive Magazine*
5 *Lowestoft Weekly Journal*
6 *The Railway Magazine*